The Victorian Novel

Barbara Dennis

Series Editor: Adrian Barlow

CAMBRIDGE
UNIVERSITY PRESS

PUBLISHED BY THE PRESS SYNDICATE OF THE UNIVERSITY OF CAMBRIDGE
The Pitt Building, Trumpington Street, Cambridge, United Kingdom

CAMBRIDGE UNIVERSITY PRESS
The Edinburgh Building, Cambridge CB2 2RU, UK
40 West 20th Street, New York, NY 10011–4211, USA
10 Stamford Road, Oakleigh, VIC 3166, Australia
Ruiz de Alarcón 13, 28014 Madrid, Spain
Dock House, The Waterfront, Cape Town 8001, South Africa

http://www.cambridge.org

First published 2000

Printed in the United Kingdom at the University Press, Cambridge

Typefaces: Clearface and Mixage   *System:* QuarkXPress® 4.1

A catalogue record for this book is available from the British Library

Acknowledgements

The author and publishers wish to thank the following for permission to use copyright material:

London Management on behalf of the Estate of the author for Max Beerbohm 'A Feast' from *A Christmas Garland*, Heinemann (1912). Copyright © the Estate of Max Beerbohm; Routledge for material from Arnold Kettle *An Introduction to the English Novel*, Unwin Hyman (1951).
Every effort has been made to reach copyright holders; the publishers would like to hear from anyone whose rights they have unknowingly infringed.

ISBN 0 521 77595 7 paperback

Prepared for publication by Gill Stacey
Designed by Tattersall Hammarling & Silk
Cover illustration: *Love Sonnets*, 1894 (w/c on paper) by Marie Spantali Stillman (1844–1927), Delaware Art Museum/Visual Arts Library/Bridgeman Art Library. Samuel and Mary R. Bancroft Memorial.

Contents

Introduction

When Queen Victoria came to the throne in 1837 the novel was barely past its infancy. Fiction had existed as long as human consciousness, of course (Neanderthal Man, E.M. Forster assures us, listened to stories), but the novel – 'fiction in prose of a certain length', to give it one classic, hold-all definition – really dates back no further than the 18th century. Earlier fiction, the 16th-century tales and romances of Nash and Dekker, can sooner be defined as pamphlets; and John Bunyan and Jonathan Swift, though they wrote extensive and entertaining narratives, must be defined by their motives for writing and seen as writers of allegory and satire. But when Daniel Defoe published *Robinson Crusoe* in 1719, and Samuel Richardson, Henry Fielding and Tobias Smollett followed with works like *Pamela*, *Joseph Andrews* and *Roderick Random*, a new convention was born.

The new form took as its topic (broadly speaking) the nature of the individual and his/her relationship with society, and investigated the variety of human experience and the responses of individual characters to it. And by the end of the 18th century the novel was so far advanced in form that a new writer, Jane Austen, could describe it famously as 'a work in which the most thorough knowledge of human nature, the happiest delineation of its varieties, the liveliest effusions of wit and humour, are conveyed to the world in the best chosen language'. She was writing in particular, it seems, of the women novelists, who were by then among the most notable contributors to the new form – as they continued to be in the next century. This book will examine the role of women in the development of the novel, and assess the significance of their contribution.

The novel in the 19th century

Jane Austen and Sir Walter Scott took the new form into the new century and, though very different artists, both continued the interest in the individual consciousness which had characterised the previous generation, and from which the Victorians were to learn and develop. But by 1837 the novel was in the hands of the young Charles Dickens, who had become a household name almost overnight with *The Pickwick Papers*, serialised in 1836–1837. This book will consider the significance of serial publication in this period, a convention popular with both publishers and the growing reading public, and the format for the appearance of a great number of Victorian novels.

Following swiftly, in the 1840s appeared a whole generation of writers who virtually created the genus 'the Victorian novel' – Dickens was joined by novelists like Thackeray, Charlotte Brontë, Emily Brontë, Benjamin Disraeli, Elizabeth Gaskell, and others. Names as distinguished followed after (Anthony Trollope,

Wilkie Collins, George Eliot), and a myriad of lesser names. Notable writers like Thomas Hardy, George Meredith, and Henry James, were also on the stage or in the wings; and by the time Queen Victoria celebrated her Golden Jubilee in 1887 the novel had become the most sophisticated art form of the century. It was also a major source of commentary on the country that ruled the largest empire in the world. This book will investigate how far this was seen as an important function of the novel, and what purpose it served.

By the end of the century, however, the novel had begun to reflect the self-consciousness and growing unease of a society no longer so secure in the pre-eminent position it had enjoyed in the middle decades of the century, as the world moved towards 1914 and the end of all things Victorian.

The novel and society

The first real burgeoning of the novel in the 1840s had coincided with a decade particularly significant in the development of British society. The prosperity of the country, which was the result of Britain's position at the global centre of economic productivity, had also resulted in social distress in the new cities on a scale never before experienced, and extracted a high price in human terms. While the rich (the middle-class capitalist masters of the system) grew richer, the poor (the workforce on which national economic success finally depended) grew poorer. The rising population surged into the new industrial cities in search of work, transported by the railways which had begun to revolutionise travel, and the agricultural economy of a thousand years became one that depended on industry and the productivity of the 'Workshop of the World'. The 'Condition-of-England' novel, examining these social, economic and political upheavals, played a significant part in confirming the popularity and significance of the novel in the 1840s.

At the same time, the novel as a form developed widely in other directions too. With its now established concerns for the relationship between the individual and society, it mirrored the significant developments in social history; it was also a recorder of the 'Victorian values' proposed by the middle class. The concern of the novel with the individual victims of industrial society, and, at the same time, the value system promoted by the middle classes, will both be investigated in the course of this book. Other types of novel about the different areas in society, such as the church, politics, the Empire, and so on, and the attitudes of mind behind them, will be examined too. The Utilitarian philosophy, which governed so much of the Victorian age, will also be the focus of enquiry here.

It was not only the poor, the victims of contemporary ideology, who provided the material for the novelists: by far the larger number of novels dealt with the constantly increasing mass of individuals who made up, or aspired to make up, the middle class. Social mobility was another pervasive theme in the novel, and is examined here.

The novel and the individual

In a further development (though the stages overlap) the focus moved from the rise of the middle class and the establishment of Victorian values to a closer concern with the psychological identity of individual characters, and how they reacted to the changes in society. Now the action tended to take place in the mind of the individual as much as in the contextual events. Then, in the latter part of the century the novel moved into what many consider to be its greatest phase with the later work of Dickens and George Eliot, and the novels of Meredith, Hardy and James. They all, and others who achieved less recognition, used the novel to provide a commentary on the society in which they lived, and saw this (to a greater or lesser degree) as their motive for writing. This book invites readers to reflect on the whole phenomenon of the Victorian novel and its role in dissecting and informing the society which produced it; to this end the focus will necessarily include the work of its lesser-known as well as its most famous novelists. The reasons for the growth of the novel, and its spectacular success, will be examined and discussed.

How this book is organised

Part 1: Approaching the Victorian novel

Part 1 begins with an introduction to the Victorian age, followed by a survey of the Victorian novel in relation to the political, social, religious and cultural movements of the era.

Part 2: Approaching the texts

Part 2 is concerned with key issues connected with the Victorian novel: why were novels so popular during the period? What is meant by 'the author'? What is the relationship between author and reader? What are the conventions of the Victorian novel?

Part 3: Texts and extracts

Part 3 contains a selection of passages from Victorian novels and essays discussed elsewhere in the book or designed for use as the focus of tasks and assignments. Some of the material included in this Part will be unfamiliar to most readers and will help to provide a broader understanding of the range of Victorian fiction.

Part 4: Critical approaches

Part 4 examines the way in which attitudes towards the Victorian novel changed and developed during the 20th century. It explores the idea of a canon of Victorian fiction and raises questions about the different ways in which a novel can be read.

Part 5: How to write about the Victorian novel

Part 5 offers guidelines and assignments for those for whom this book is chiefly intended: students covering the topic as part of an advanced course in literary studies.

Part 6: Resources

Part 6 contains a chronology of texts and authors discussed in this book, together with guidance on further reading, and a glossary and index. (Terms which appear in the glossary are highlighted in bold type throughout the book.)

At different points throughout the book, and at the end of Parts 1, 2, 4 and 5, there are tasks and assignments which suggest a variety of contexts through which students might approach an understanding of particular works.

1 | Approaching the Victorian novel

- What does 'Victorian' mean?

- What are the main subjects of the Victorian novel?

- How does the Victorian novel reflect the social attitudes of its writers and its original readers?

- How does the novel develop during the course of the 19th century?

> Nothing is so likely to recruit the exhausted powers of our [novelists] as the admission of fresh air from the outer world. There is no lack of fit subjects. Themes of public interest are certainly not wanting ... The practical and religious issues of our time are not less momentous than [in the 17th century] ...
>
> *(Quarterly Review*, 1875)

> For any detailed description of the complexity of human nature, ... of the multifarious play of the social environment on the individual ego and of the individual ego on the social environment, I had to turn to novelists ...
>
> (Beatrice Webb *My Apprenticeship*, 1926)

The Victorian scene

'It was the best of times, it was the worst of times', as Charles Dickens had put it. He was speaking of the years surrounding the French Revolution of 1789, but he added that the time was so far like his own era as to be different only in degree. A century after the Victorian age it is possible to see more readily and to focus more clearly on the extremes which characterised the 19th century. With the advantage of hindsight, the reader can reconcile the different views presented by, on the one hand, Lord Macaulay (who saw 'nothing but improvement' wherever he looked) and on the other Thomas Carlyle (who thought we were 'all going straight away to the dogs').

It is difficult to generalise confidently about a period which covers the best part of a century, but even by the 1840s what was striking commentators was the speed, hitherto unparalleled, with which the world was changing in political, social, scientific, ecclesiastical developments. In the first half of the century, it is certainly true that as a nation Britain led the western world in the advance towards industrialisation, and had reaped the benefits in the national prosperity which ensued. Until at least the 1870s Britain was economically supreme. To a large extent this had been brought about by the gradual introduction, by a series of Prime Ministers, of free trade – the abolition, or reduction, of duty on raw materials like wool and cotton, and a variety of manufactured goods. The **Manchester School** of economic thought, which believed in freeing commerce from all trammels, was so successful that by 1860 William Ewart Gladstone, who was then Chancellor, could agree 'We have as much prosperity as we can bear'. The Great Exhibition of 1851, in the Crystal Palace, was a monument to the confidence of British trade and industry, and a personal triumph for Prince Albert, whose brainchild it had partly been. It bore witness to the lead that Britain had established in specialised production and technological invention, a position that was maintained until the recessions that set in during the 1870s.

The 'Two Nations'

It is equally true that the national prosperity, obvious in the ironworks, the pits and the factories which were covering the country as the new towns grew and spread, was not reflected in the squalid back-to-back housing in which the workforce lived, nor in the pinched, starved faces of the unemployed. The owners and employers who enjoyed the 'improvements' that Lord Macaulay boasted of, spoke with pride of the achievements of England and ploughed the profits back in fresh investment, while the working men and women struggled, sometimes in vain, for bare subsistence, and viewed with resentment the different lot of the 'masters'. Benjamin Disraeli, not yet Prime Minister, summed it up famously in his novel *Sybil* (1845) when he spoke of the Two Nations:

> Two nations; between whom there is no intercourse and no sympathy; who are as ignorant of each other's habits, thoughts, and feelings, as if they were dwellers in different zones, or inhabitants of different planets; who were formed by different breeding, are fed by different food, are ordered by different manners, and are not governed by the same laws ... THE RICH AND THE POOR.

Working-class unrest: the Chartist Movement

Disraeli, and several other novelists, gave their own account of the civil unrest which seemed to threaten the country, partly as a result of the yawning divide between the classes, in the middle decades of the century. The beginnings of organised labour had appeared with the London Working Men's Association in 1836, and the **Chartist Movement** was established in Birmingham in 1838, with the 'People's Charter' of six points: a vote for all adult males, equal electoral districts, payment of MPs, abolition of property qualifications for MPs, a secret ballot and annual elections. These six points were all intended to make the British system of voting and parliamentary representation fairer and less biased in favour of the property- and business-owning classes. But the Charter was – predictably – overwhelmingly rejected by Parliament in 1839, and a second petition was thrown out in 1842. A third mass demonstration in 1848 seriously alarmed the authorities, who feared that the revolutions which had rocked Europe were to be re-enacted on these shores, but this too collapsed ingloriously in the pouring rain, and the movement for parliamentary reform became less militant.

Parliamentary reform

The first parliamentary reform had come with the Great **Reform Bill** of 1832, which had done nothing for working-class voters, but had given some representation to the new urban centres, and had opened the door a crack for further reforming legislation. This followed in 1867, and the Second Reform Bill was much more democratic in effect, practically doubling the electorate and enfranchising many of the lower middle class. A third, of 1884, added more voters to the electorate; and all but one (annual parliaments) of the Chartists' original demands had by now been met. The currents and tensions of the contemporary political reforming programme are mirrored in the novel, memorably in George Eliot's Felix *Holt the Radical* (1866) which, though set in the time of the 1832 Reform Bill, is informed by what was happening in the 1860s.

Other reforms

Social reform followed parliamentary reform as both **Whig** and **Tory** administrations embarked on a programme of Factory Acts, Mines Acts, and even the beginnings of educational reform, in the 1830s and 1840s. Among these possibly the most significant and far-reaching was the **Poor Law Amendment Act** of 1834. This was one of the most important documents in 19th-century history, about which Dickens wrote so notably in the opening chapters of *Oliver Twist* (1838): the re-ordering of the workhouses, and the fear they inspired in the working classes, permeate the pages of much Victorian fiction.

Utilitarianism

The measures of the Prime Ministers, Lord Grey, Lord Melbourne, and then Robert Peel, were rarely hailed as the last word in reforming zeal: the poor were often more aware of what seemed the inhumanity of these new systems than of how they were likely to improve the human condition. Indeed, the motives behind the new legislation were often based less on humanitarian sentiment than on strict principles of economy and on the philosophy of Jeremy Bentham.

Jeremy Bentham had died as the Great Reform Bill reached the statute books in 1832, but the influence of his thinking spread through society for the rest of the century. Benthamism, or **Utilitarianism**, was a philosophic system which tested all the institutions of social life by the criterion of their usefulness – his question was always not 'How old is it?' but 'What use is it?' and he evaluated usefulness by quantifying the happiness ('the greatest happiness of the greatest number') which resulted. Few of the Victorian men and women who came to be thought of as Utilitarians, however, were actively conscious of subscribing to the set of beliefs concerning the nature of man, the meaning of freedom, and so on, which characterise the rest of Bentham's philosophic position: they selected from Bentham the strands of thought which seemed to confirm their own instincts and prejudices, and their vocabulary of *laissez-faire* and individual self-interest (catch-phrases of Utilitarianism) was really a rationalisation of this.

It was a philosophy which seemed to reduce the individual and individuality to insignificance. The most important attack on Utilitarianism in action is found in Dickens' novel *Hard Times* (1854):

> You saw nothing in Coketown but what was severely workful. If the members of a religious persuasion built a chapel there – as the members of eighteen religious persuasions had done – they made it a pious warehouse of red brick. ... Fact, fact, fact, everywhere in the material aspect of the town; fact, fact, fact, everywhere in the immaterial. The M'Choakumchild school was all fact, and the school of design was all fact, and everything was fact between the lying-in hospital [the maternity hospital] and the cemetery, and what you couldn't state in figures, or show to be puchasable in the cheapest market and saleable in the dearest, was not, and never should be, world without end, Amen.

▶ Look at the way Dickens defines Utilitarianism and expresses his attitude towards it in this passage, without ever using the actual word. How does the language and imagery he employs suggest that Utilitarianism has become a false religion?

The influence of Carlyle

Most of the 'masters', the millowners, employers and shareholders who profited from Britain's lead in the Industrial Revolution, can be seen as Utilitarians in this sense, and literature is littered with portraits of them. In *Hard Times*, Dickens introduced Bounderby and Mr Gradgrind, and George Eliot offered Bulstrode in *Middlemarch* (1871–1872). Anticipating them all, Thomas Carlyle had created Plugson of Undershot in *Past and Present* (1843), a commentary on cultural thinking in which he warns of the dangers of an increasingly mechanised society. (There is an extract from the book in Part 3, pages 70–71.)

Plugson, though he is not a character in a novel, provides a model for all novelists to follow. Carlyle, Dickens and George Eliot remind readers that there was always a section of the educated middle class who were articulate thinkers. They presented the human side of the Industrial Revolution: in their work they examined the 'Condition-of England Question' (Carlyle's phrase) to expose the underside of society. Many of them offered their own solutions to the problems they discerned at the heart of the community, and as often as not they looked back to the past for the answers.

This past was not the immediate past, for the 18th century, with its heartless attitudes and unfeeling views, seemed to these writers to be the age which had spawned the worst features of their own; instead they looked back to the comfortably remote Middle Ages. They saw the pre-Reformation years of the 13th and 14th centuries as the time when society was an organic whole, held together by a common religion and an acknowledged social order; and the storm-tossed Victorians looked back wistfully to this never-never land in their literature and art, and sought to re-create at least the outward signs of it in their Gothic revival architecture. Carlyle in particular was responsible for so many of the mid-century attitudes, and numbers of the novelists of the middle decades of the century were quite open about their debt to him. The novels of Dickens, Elizabeth Gaskell, Disraeli and George Eliot are obvious examples. In his *History of the French Revolution* (1837) Carlyle had seemed to warn of the danger of social revolution spreading to England; in *Hard Times*, the mill-owner Bounderby and his friend Gradgrind assert that the working people of Coketown were

> a bad lot altogether, gentlemen; that do what you would for them they were never thankful for it, gentlemen; that they were restless, gentlemen … that they were eternally dissatisfied and unmanageable.

Dickens argues in the novel that the Gradgrind principles by which the people have been educated and by which they now work are responsible for their discontent. He sees this as understandable, even though he feels as much threatened by social disorder as Bounderby does. Dickens' proposal in *Hard Times* is for a new type of education – one which will nurture the imagination as much as the intellect.

Education

Education was one of the solutions Carlyle was firm in advocating, and the novelists echoed him: as democracy became more and more of a fact after the 1867 Reform Act, the necessity to 'educate our masters' grew more pressing. Primary education for all was finally instituted by the **Education Act** of 1870. The need for education in a wider sense was pressed on the public by writers like Matthew

Arnold, and the novelists, too, saw their role as public educators.

Before 1870 provision of schooling was extremely patchy, often depending on whether a local school had been established in the town or village by an earlier benefactor, or whether there was a church school. National Schools were organised by the Church of England; British Schools by the Nonconformist churches. When Jane Eyre, in Charlotte Brontë's novel, establishes a little dame school for the local children, there is a glimpse of just how random the provision of schooling really was.

The Empire

British colonialism expanded at such a rate in Victoria's reign that by the end of the century Britain ruled one tenth of the earth's surface. The stimulus to this growth was trade ('Trade follows the flag' was a popular dictum of 19th-century Imperialism), for the expanding industries at home needed outlets for their products, and fresh supplies of raw materials. The Empire – in India, Africa, Australia, Canada – was largely won, governed and administered by the younger sons of the middle classes who (at the urging of Carlyle, and others) went out to seek fresh fields of colonial trade, colonial administration, colonial education, and so on. There can have been few families with no contact, in some form or another, with the Empire – all ranks served overseas in the armed services, for instance. And in novel after novel the influence of the Imperial experience is reflected, often so casually that it is scarcely obvious – the expected return of a traveller, for instance, or a gift from overseas. But a whole school of novelists, especially later in the century, make the Empire the central focus of their **discourse**. For this reason, post-colonial criticism takes a particular interest in the Victorian novel.

It is, however, also important to bear in mind that the anti-slavery movement of the early 19th century had had a significant influence on public opinion towards the Empire, particularly Africa. **Evangelical** activists such as William Wilberforce, George Clarkson and Isaac Watts had done much to provoke a more questioning attitude towards Britain's relationship with the colonies and their inhabitants.

Religion

Ideas of reform and change permeated every element of society, including the ecclesiastical. The century had opened in the wake of a major Evangelical revival, seen clearly in the upsurge of Methodism and the teaching of John and Charles Wesley. Then in 1833 came the **Oxford Movement**, which reminded the Anglican Church of its pre-Reformation roots, and which continued to affect society well into the 20th century. The Roman Catholics too, who had been granted full civic rights in 1829 but were traditionally regarded with suspicion, flourished as never since the Reformation of the 16th century. Their numbers were inflated by the waves of immigrants from Ireland and, in the 1840s and 1850s, by the stream of converts who left the Church of England as a result of the Oxford Movement. Meanwhile the **Nonconformists** grew increasingly in importance: the **Test Acts** which had handicapped them since 1698 were repealed in 1828; they were largely enfranchised (given the right to vote) by the 1867 Reform Bill, and among their numbers were many of the leading factory owners and industrial magnates responsible for British commercial supremacy.

Though the age was, therefore – in any outward sense – the most religious ever seen in Britain (nearly all the Nonconformist churches still standing belong to this period, and half the parish churches), it was also an era of religious doubt, when all the certainties of Christianity were called in question as new knowledge about science and history and the Bible was thrust before the public eye. 'Infidel' was the old word that society applied to those who had no faith, and the open unbeliever was not made welcome in respectable society; but now it was not merely rakes and philosophers who challenged revealed truth, but a significant number of thinking people, and a new word – 'agnostic'- was coined to cover those who wrestled, often with confusion and dismay, with the problems that beset Victorian religion. Representatives of all schools of religious thought, of all church parties and of none, appear in the novel as the novelists, including Dickens, the Brontës, George Eliot and Elizabeth Gaskell, reflected the world they lived in.

The novel and the middle class

From its beginning the novel has looked to society for its themes: social experience has always been the source from which it has drawn its material. In the Victorian period two of the great themes of the novel are the depiction and analysis of society as a whole, and the adjustment of the individual to this society. Victorian society was seen to be shaped and formed by individuals: it followed therefore that the emphasis of the novel was on 'characters', who would reflect the 'Victorian values' on which society was based, self-help, self-dependency – and success.

But throughout the period society was in a state of flux as every part was invented or re-invented. As early as 1831, John Stuart Mill, in *The Spirit of the Age*, was claiming:

> The first of the leading peculiarities of the present age is, that it is an age of transition. Mankind have outgrown old institutions and doctrines, and have not yet acquired new ones.

With the change in institutions, the expansion of professions, and the re-distribution of wealth, the middle class grew and became more obviously important. The novel, which had always tended to reflect society – itself in the hands of the educated, literate middle class – recorded this.

The values presented and endorsed in the novel are those of the middle class, at least in the earlier Victorian period. The ideal society to which the characters aspire is bourgeois: success is customarily seen in terms of money and the status which accompanies it.

The novel and the bourgeois ethic: *Oliver Twist* and *Wuthering Heights*

A central theme in the Victorian novel is the adjustment of the main character to a middle-class world, and his/her approval by middle-class opinion. For example, in *Oliver Twist* (1837–1838), Oliver makes his way from a humble and disadvantaged position to acceptance and approval by middle-class respectability: Oliver's story takes him from the pauper conditions of the workhouse, through his apprenticeship as a pickpocket in Bill Sikes's gang, to his rescue and redemption by first Mr Brownlow and then Rose Maylie – and finally to the discovery that, after all, by birth he belongs safely to the middle class.

It is a key theme, of course, in Emily Brontë's *Wuthering Heights* (1847), where the question is discussed from a rather different angle, when the suburban values of the middle-class Lintons are confronted by the elemental passions of Heathcliff. Catherine Earnshaw is the initial conduit between the two. When, at the age of twelve, Catherine is transformed by the Lintons from a 'wild, hatless little savage' into a socially acceptable young lady, the young, tough Heathcliff is excluded. It is his description of what he sees as the meretricious values of Thrushcross Grange (the Linton's family home) that is reported back to Wuthering Heights. He describes 'a splendid place carpeted with crimson, and crimson-covered chairs and tables, and a pure white ceiling bordered with gold, a shower of glass drops hanging on silver chains from the centre ...', but with the children Edgar and Isabella quarrelling violently over a puppy and 'yelling and sobbing and rolling on the ground'.

But Catherine is seduced by the conventional world of the gentry, and ends by marrying the effete, but gentlemanly, Edgar. Heathcliff is emotionally untouched by the bourgeois **ideology** of the Linton world, but he loses Catherine to it.

The chief narrator in the novel is Lockwood, from the same class as the Lintons, but who reports the family history as told to him by a servant, the housekeeper Nellie. Though the overall viewpoint is Lockwood's, it is not the authorial viewpoint. The middle-class consciousness which directs *Oliver Twist* is not obvious here; nonetheless, Emily Brontë records the pervasive spread of the bourgeois ethic just as faithfully as does Dickens.

The search for identity: *Great Expectations* and *Jane Eyre*

The search for identity is another important theme in the Victorian novel, a theme which overlaps continually with that of individual adjustment to society. Many novels of this time concern the hero's or heroine's life as he/she journeys from one stage to the next in the quest for 'self'. Dickens, as always, provides excellent examples, especially in the earlier novels, and as well as *Oliver Twist*, *Nicholas Nickleby* (1838–1839) and *David Copperfield* (1849–1850) follow the fortunes of the central characters in their struggles to define themselves. (There is an extract from *David Copperfield* on pages 74–75.)

Dickens' motive here was not simple endorsement of the middle-class ethic: as his work matured, he was to call into question every aspiration of the money-obsessed society he lived in, and to present a savage indictment of its commercial values. By the time he wrote *Great Expectations* in 1861, the life-journey of Pip from a humble background to a haven of middle-class respectability offered by his 'expectations' was ostensibly a familiar one. But Dickens' intention in this novel is different: while Oliver Twist prospers in his middle-class environment, Pip's triumph is to reject the ideals of that world and to return to his roots with Joe and Biddy in the village of his childhood. Pip, certainly, learns more on his journey through life than simply the values of an acquisitive society. With Joe as his unconscious mentor, Pip learns humanity and genuine good feeling – and the final irrelevance of what Miss Havisham has taught him at Satis House. Like Estella, he has been 'bent and broken, but ... into a better shape'.

There are many famous examples of this kind of ***Bildungsroman*** (as these novels of education, or youthful development are often known). Charlotte Brontë uses similar techniques in her novels, in particular in *Jane Eyre* (1847) and *Villette* (1853).

Jane Eyre is a novel of the inner life, depicting Jane's voyage of self-discovery. As Jane moves from the breakfast-room at Gateshead where she is tormented by John Reed, and the Red Room, where she is driven by fear almost to the point of mental breakdown, to Mr Brocklehurst's Lowood, to Thornfield, and to Moor House, the reader is not so much concerned with the outward events of her life as with what is happening inside her head in her passionate search for her destiny. It is her sense of herself which predominates throughout (as the extract in Part 3, pages 71–72, illustrates). When Rochester wears down her resolve almost to breaking point after the farcical wedding ceremony, and Feeling urges 'Oh, comply!' with his demands that she be his mistress, Jane's sturdy sense of herself resists: 'Still indomitable was the reply – I care for myself. The more solitary, the more friendless, the more unsustained I am, the more I will respect myself ...'. At the end of the novel, she resolves the quest for her identity in the triumphant 'Reader, I married him' – on her terms.

The question of the gentleman

Pip and the nature of his 'great expectations' illustrates another theme in the Victorian novel which overlaps significantly with both the search for identity and the expansion of the middle class: the definition of a gentleman. It was a question the Victorians probed and debated and discussed endlessly. With the growing democratisation of society came a growing tide of debate about the 'gentleman' – his definition, his nature, his function – as old ideas about traditional hierarchy were challenged and exploded. As society changed shape with the new professions created by the Industrial Revolution (for example, careers afforded by new developments in engineering, technology, and so on) and the reforms which changed the structures of the army, the church, the civil service, etc., familiar class distinctions were breaking down and raising questions about the nature of divisions in society. In this new urban-based civilisation there was no longer a peasantry, the middle class was expanding infinitely, and the aristocracy was no longer recruited solely from traditional landowners.

All this made excellent material for the novelist, and, from the mid-century, an examination of the question of the gentleman became a regular theme in the novel. Samuel Smiles, the enormously popular author of *Self-Help* (1859), codified the ideology of the self-made man, who might rise from humble origins to riches by means of diligence and prudence. Smiles' doctrine of self-help assumed a world in which social advancement is both possible and desirable. He stressed that 'Riches and rank have no necessary connection with genuine gentlemanly qualities. The poor man may be a true gentleman – in spirit and in daily life. He may be honest, truthful, upright, polite, temperate, courageous, self-respecting, and self-helping – that is, a true gentleman.'

Dinah Mulock's novel, *John Halifax, Gentleman* (1857), is the story of how John Halifax, born in poverty, rises from a destitute life in the gutter to become through diligence and honesty a popular local employer, blissfully married to a daughter of the gentry. John Halifax is *Self-Help* fictionalised, he follows every detail prescribed by Smiles: he has natural courtesy, natural consideration, natural self-respect, and knows himself from the beginning to be the equal of any lord. (There is an extract from the novel on pages 78–79.)

Anthony Trollope makes a case for a more traditional version of the gentleman in *The Way We Live Now* (1875). Here Roger Carbury stands for the old ideal and the stability of the old order, where birth, class, rank and property are the foundations on which the social edifice stands. They are threatened by the new world of Melmotte (of no origin, no background and of dubious reputation) whose fortune, it seems, supersedes every other qualification for a gentleman. For Trollope (as for Dickens, who created a similar character, Merdle, in *Little Dorrit*) Melmotte lacked every qualification for a gentleman, which was not a degree to be bought for money. (There is an extract from the novel on pages 82–84.)

All the same, it was a question which occupied the Victorians – could the condition of 'gentleman' be sold to the highest bidder? Dickens considers the question roundly in *Great Expectations*: Pip, when he assumes that it is the leisured, wealthy Miss Havisham's money on which he can base his expectations, is eager to become what he sees as a gentleman and to distance himself from life at the forge with Joe. Only when he discovers that his benefactor is the convict Magwitch who, like Pip, assumes that the qualities of a gentleman lie in surface appearances, and can be bought, does he realise his mistake. 'I was making a gentleman', says Magwitch when he explains the situation to Pip, 'if I aint a gentleman, nor aint got no learning, I'm the owner of such.' Pip is 'too stunned to think'.

The real gentleman in the novel is Joe, who enjoys no material advancement and remains a brave, industrious, honest blacksmith throughout, the very embodiment of moral and social virtue. Pip acknowledges as much and bitterly regrets the blindness of his snobbery, the result of his expectations. Dickens certainly questions the concept of social improvement as the definition of class, much as he had dismissed the idea of 'making a gentleman' with money.

He had raised the same question, less significantly in terms of theme, but as forcefully and pervasively, in *Little Dorrit* (1857), the novel before *Great Expectations*. This novel opens with two convicts, Rigaud and Cavaletto, in the gaol at Marseilles. Rigaud, whom the reader knows to be a villain, announces himself to be a gentleman to his fellow-prisoner. He conducts himself, as he thinks, appropriately:

> Have I ever done anything here? Ever touched the broom, or spread
> the mats, or rolled them up … or put my hand to any kind of work? …
> A gentleman I am! And a gentleman I'll die!

This is how a gentleman defines himself for Rigaud – he does not work. And Cavaletto, who is a gentleman by every item in Smiles' catalogue, if no other, and does all the work in the cell, humbly accepts Rigaud's definition. For Mr Dorrit, in another prison, the knowledge that he is a gentleman has been the mainstay of his endurance of twenty-five years in the Marshalsea. It is of enormous importance to him that the other prisoners, his 'fellow-Collegians', acknowledge that he is better born and better educated, and not as they are, that he is 'always a gentleman' – and one who, like Rigaud, does not work. In the final analysis, Mr Dorrit's idea of gentlemanliness rests on money, and the legacy which turns his fortunes confirms his status. The fashionable world, from which he is later so careful to conceal his Marshalsea experience, is, in fact, quite indifferent to his past as long as his fortune remains.

There are few gentlemen who would answer Smiles' prescription in this gloomy novel, though Dickens assembles a gallery of candidates for consideration – Sparkler, Gowan, all the Barnacles, Merdle (whose butler speaks his epitaph, 'Mr Merdle was never the gentleman, and no ungentlemanly act on Mr Merdle's part would surprise me ...'), etc. Perhaps Young John Chivery, son of the turnkey, comes nearest to it: though 'his exterior had very much of a turnkey about it, and not the least of a gentleman', he always acts with 'native delicacy' and 'true politeness'. His unwelcome gift of cigars after Mr Dorrit has moved on from his 'college life' comes from a heart 'too proud and honourable' to behave in any other way.

The industrial scene

The most obvious – certainly the most visible – of the signs of change in society were brought about by the Industrial Revolution. For the first time, the visibly changing face of England, with its smoke and grime, its sprawling new towns, its factories and mills and the suffering that went with them, became the subject matter of literature.

Carlyle had prepared the ground with his savage attacks on the attitudes of mind which promoted middle-class greed, and an important group of novelists followed him in the 1840s and 1850s. The novels of Dickens, Disraeli, Elizabeth Gaskell, even Charlotte Brontë, offer the imaginative response to the distress and poverty behind the apparent prosperity of society – and a portrayal of the Industrial Revolution in human terms.

The industrial novel: *Mary Barton*

Among the first, and most effective, of these writers was Elizabeth Gaskell, who published *Mary Barton* in 1848 – and who acknowledged her debt to Carlyle on the title page. Of all the novelists, she is the only one who, as it were, lived on the job: married to a Unitarian minister in Manchester, she passed her daily life among the people and the scenes which make up the novel. When famine was rife in Manchester as a result of the cotton-strikes of the early 1860s, Elizabeth Gaskell and her daughter were at the forefront of the volunteers who brought succour to the needy.

But mere social worker's interest is never enough for Elizabeth Gaskell: her engagement with, and respect for, her characters are too genuine. *Mary Barton* (and, a little later, *North and South*) is eloquent about the appalling, almost incredible, poverty and murderous resentment that abounded in the Manchester slums. Yet the novelist sees the problem as lying not in what she called 'Political Economy' but in human failings. Her attack is directed less against the whole system of industrial capitalism than against what she sees as the ignorance that lies between the rich and the poor – and her answer is to promote communication between the classes. She believes in the basic goodness of human nature and the ability of humankind to solve life's problems, given good will and good intentions. So at the deathbed of John Barton (the Chartist leader who has murdered his employer's son), Mr Carson, the factory owner, is finally persuaded to extend forgiveness:

> He raised up the powerless frame; and the departing soul looked out of the eyes with gratitude. He held the dying man propped up in his arms. John Barton folded his hands as if in prayer.
> 'Pray for us', said Mary, sinking to her knees and forgetting in that solemn hour all that had divided her father and Mr Carson.
> No other words would suggest themselves than some of those he had read only a few hours before.
> 'God be merciful to us sinners. – Forgive us our trespasses as we forgive them that trespass against us.'

Elizabeth Gaskell has no sympathy with Chartism as such, and sees the point of view of the employer as well as the employed. In the Preface to *Mary Barton*, she stresses that she is not interested in 'Political Economy or the theories of trade', and that her motive in writing is 'to give some utterance to the agony which, from time to time, convulses this dumb people', those 'doomed to struggle through their lives in strange alternatives between work and want'.

Her interest is not in the system but in the individuals caught up in it, be they masters or men. In a reflective coda which follows the drama of the deathbed, the dialogue between Mr Carson and Job Legh, the wise elder statesman of the working community, makes her position clear. Job Legh tells the factory owner that a major part of John Barton's quarrel with the system was what he saw as the masters' indifference to the plight of the workers – 'the want of inclination to try and help the evils which come like blights at times over the manufacturing places'. Carson explains the powerlessness of the masters caught up in 'events which God alone can control', but Job Legh has the last word, and it is Gaskell's: one master thereafter strove 'that a perfect understanding, and complete confidence and love, might exist between masters and men', and that men should be bound to their employers by the ties of respect and affection, not by 'mere money bargains alone'.

In the first half of *Mary Barton*, Gaskell shows herself to be a great novelist in the passionate sincerity with which she puts her case for humanitarian involvement and understanding. The picture she gives of working-class community life, and her knowledge and appreciation of its values, its decency and its dignity, were unique in early Victorian fiction, and instantly gave her a status and authority. No other imaginative account gives so vivid an understanding of what it was like to live the destitute life of the industrial poor. Her own involvement with the issues is clear throughout, as the frequent earnest authorial intrusions and commentary demonstrate, and it is implied even when the **omniscient narrator** is silent.

This is 'fiction with a purpose', and the techniques she employs to convey her message are straightforward. The abundance of detail and the photographic **realism** of the novel have always been recognised as notable characteristics, but it is also worth noting that this is part of her scheme to promote communication between the classes. The camera's-eye view of the poorest parts of Manchester and its inhabitants, and the close-ups of their culture, were a conscious effort to close the gap between the classes. John Barton declares in the opening chapter:

> Don't think to come over me with the old tale, that the rich know nothing of the trials of the poor ... I say, if they don't know, they ought to know ... [W]e pile up their fortunes with the sweat of our brows; and yet we are to live as separate ... as if we were in two worlds ... with a great gulf between us ...

Gaskell's technique is to juxtapose the contrasting images of the two worlds in her attempt to bridge the gulf. Next to the grim picture of the road where the Davenports live, with its gutter running with 'slops of every description' and the foetid, dank and freezing cellar which is their home, is the picture of the Carson household, where the family of the mill owner live, and where even the servants enjoy the comfort of a roaring fire and plentiful meals. The author gives photographic pictures of the two families, the destitute Davenports, the wife 'a fainting, dead like woman' trying to breastfeed her baby, and her husband mortally ill with typhus and sinking with starvation; and the Carsons – father, son and blooming young daughter – at the 'well-spread breakfast table' in the 'luxurious library', toying with steaks and eggs and coffee. Carson is not a bad man – he is a reasonable employer – simply ignorant. He has never heard of Davenport, who has worked for him for three years, and, unthinking, will only give him a useless post-dated outpatients' order for the hospital.

Paralleled with the industrial sprawl of Manchester and the crushing experience of industrialism is the wistful memory of the rural past, and this is another example of Gaskell's technique of contrast. Alice, who came to Manchester from Cumberland nearly seventy years before, still thinks of the country as home, and returns there in her dreams, and is there at the end when her mind fails. She is a poignant reminder of the speed with which England was being transformed into the 'Workshop of the World'. The idyll of the rural past (as she remembers it) is so near and yet so far.

Dialogue is another feature of Gaskell's plan. For almost the first time an English novelist expressed extended dialogue in the common speech of regional dialect, and her account of industrial life and the culture of working folk is in the language the people spoke. To bridge the divide between the educated middle-class reader and her subject matter, she also added a glossary and notes.

▶ Benjamin Disraeli, Prime Minister of Great Britain and himself a novelist, coined the phrase 'Two Nations' to illustrate the potentially damaging divisions in society during this period. In what terms does Elizabeth Gaskell present these divisions in her novels?

The industrial novel: *Sybil*

Disraeli anticipated Elizabeth Gaskell in his determination to show the great social divisions in society in *Sybil* (1845), where he coined the memorable phrase 'The two nations ... THE RICH AND THE POOR'; but this is really the only feature that *Sybil* and *Mary Barton* have in common, for in vision and execution they are very different novels. While *Mary Barton* aims to be a sincere photographic portrayal of working-class life in Lancashire, *Sybil* is a melodramatic extravaganza, a political novel by a rising Conservative M.P. who used Parliamentary reports and documentary evidence for his material rather than first-hand observation at the workface.

This is not to say that *Sybil* is not a serious inquiry into the 'Condition-of-England Question', only that Disraeli's motives for undertaking it are different from Gaskell's, and his methods poles apart. His solutions, for instance, are political rather than social: the novel (with two others, which form a trilogy) was to promote the Young England movement, a brand of romantic Toryism calling for a reform of the nobility and looking for a benevolent aristocracy to reform the conditions of the working class. The novel presents examples of every significant area of English society in this context: the effete and outmoded aristocrat in Lord Marney; the ideal nobleman in his heir, Egremont, a younger son who is responsible, enlightened, and high-principled; St Lys who represents the ideal version of the Anglican clergy; Trafford the ideal employer; Stephen Morley the Chartist; the rural poor; the proletariat, and so on. The signs of industrial distress are to be found concentrated in the slum called Wodgate, 'the ugliest spot in England, to which neither Nature nor art had contributed a single charm'.

But Disraeli is aware of more widespread ills than those he locates in Wodgate: Gerard, Sybil's father, a Chartist and overseer at Trafford's factory, enlightens Egremont about 'the degradation of the people' generally:

There is more serfdom now than at any time since the Conquest. ...
There are great bodies of the working classes of this country nearer the

condition of brutes than they have been at any time since the Conquest. ... We have more pestilence now in England than we ever had.

Disraeli's mind and keen intelligence are everywhere, and the myriad wrongs that the poor labour under are all grist to his mill: the truck system of paying wages in goods, conditions in coal mines, the degraded life of the agricultural labourer, the miseries of industrial apprentices are all targets against which he mounts his attack. *Sybil* is, in this sense, a novel of ideas designed to make the middle-class reader think. Indeed, one of them wrote to him, 'You set forth in stirring words, in animated, striking, and truthful description the real social condition of the country, the monstrous distinction betwixt Rich-Poor.'

▶ Can you think of any 20th-century novelists who have used the novel as a vehicle for setting out a political agenda in the same way that Disraeli was doing in *Sybil*? Contrast Disraeli's exploitation of the novel as a literary form with the ways in which it is exploited by some author-politicians today.

The actual plot of *Sybil* is of less importance than the agenda it offers. Disraeli has little interest in his characters as people, merely in what they represent. Sybil, though she gives her name to the novel, is only the useful link whose marriage with Egremont, the model of the reformed aristocracy, gives colour to Disraeli's theme of the necessity of the union between the two nations. It is very much a conservative, Young England solution. Disraeli sees the answer to current problems of industrialism as lying in the feudal past, when a benevolent aristocracy acknowledged its responsibility to the workforce it employed, and the church (its clergy drawn from the ruling classes) preached the pre-Reformation gospel of the status quo, endorsing the mediaeval ranking of crown/aristocracy/church/people.

▶ How far do you think the following verse from the 19th-century hymn 'All things bright and beautiful' may have reflected the beliefs or assumptions of Victorian novelists and their readers?

The rich man in his castle,
The poor man at his gate,
God made them high and lowly,
He ordered their estate.

When Sybil protests that the future lies with the People, who have 'learnt their strength', and Gerard declares that 'the relations of the working classes of England to its privileged orders are relations of enmity', the answer comes back from Lord Valentine: 'I do not think the majority are the best judges of their own interests ...

[The aristocracy] have mainly and materially assisted in making England what it is'; and then from Egremont: 'The new generation of the aristocracy of England are not tyrants, not oppressors ... They are the natural leaders of the People.' Disraeli, in fact, saw the salvation of England as in the hands of an enlightened aristocracy who, with the best interests of the people at heart, guide and govern like feudal lords. And Trafford, the ideal employer, is a model of this paternalistic direction. He 'had imbibed ... a correct conception of the relations which should subsist between the employer and the employed. He felt that there should be other ties than the payment and receipt of wages', and Disraeli heartily endorses this pre-industrial, anti-Utilitarian position.

Though this is an important argument in the novel, what holds *Sybil* together is Disraeli's personality and the play of his mind as he moves restlessly from one idea to the next. He is more obviously at home in the London clubs and parliamentary gatherings than in the squalor of Wodgate (the details of which are painstakingly assembled from government reports), but even here he infuses his narrative with consistent wit and vitality.

Religion

Probably no period in English history has been so religious – or at least thought as much about religion – as the Victorian. What you believed, what you didn't believe, mattered tremendously. It affected every area of life, public and private, social, political, educational, professional. The pervasive spirit of reform and change which was sweeping through society was felt as much in ecclesiastical areas as in all the others; inevitably the novel reflects this.

The Evangelical revival

Organised religion had been swept by the great Evangelical revival headed by John Wesley (1703–1791) and his brother Charles (1707–1788) in the previous century, which resulted in the foundation of Methodism; and a similar revival was later felt in the Church of England (a church which the Wesleys never left). William Wilberforce (1759–1833) and Lord Shaftesbury (1801–1885) are the names most associated with this branch of the Evangelical Movement: the emphasis of the movement on good works was most prominent in the great social reforms for which they are best known. The faith of the Evangelicals was intensely personal, and was expressed in strict standards of conduct – good works were an essential part of their code. They were less concerned with outward religious observances than with inward 'vital religion', a deeply felt belief in the redemption of man from his sinful state made possible through Christ's death.

Evangelicalism was very much the religion of the burgeoning middle class who were beginning to run Victorian society. It was a religion which could be easily appropriated by the self-made businessmen who readily acknowledged what they saw as the link between their economic individualism and the deeply personal nature of Evangelical religion (and divine approval could be inferred from the soaring profits which so often resulted). It identified clearly with the prevailing Utilitarian ethic.

Evangelicals and the novel: *Little Dorrit* and *Middlemarch*

There are many portraits of such Evangelicals in the novel, often satirical (for the inherent possibilities for self-deception and hypocrisy offered irresistible opportunities to the satirist), but sometimes seriously thoughtful. Dickens offers a gallery of satirical likenesses of the Evangelical school – Mr Chadband in *Bleak House* (1853), Mr Podsnap in *Our Mutual Friend* (1865) and Mr Pecksniff in *Martin Chuzzlewit* (1844) are merely three of many. There is another example in Miss Clack, the Evangelical busybody, in Wilkie Collins' *The Moonstone*.

Dickens gives a different kind of portrait in the full-length study of the Evangelical school in Mrs Clennam in *Little Dorrit*. Mrs Clennam is the very embodiment of everything negative about the Evangelical religion. Her son Arthur's vision of the joyless Sunday includes the image of his mother, 'stern of face and unrelenting of heart', reading her Bible (ornamented by a chain) all day and tracing in it the hardest and narrowest interpretations of punishment and torment. All her reading is from the Old Testament: Mrs Clennam justifies her obsession with 'reparation and restitution' by reference to the grimmest books there, and ignores the forgiving message of Christ in the New Testament. Her religion is personal and based on her – selective – study of the Bible, and is part of the imprisonment which is the dominant image of the novel.

George Eliot presents a serious study of this religious school in Mr Tryan in 'Janet's Repentance' in *Scenes of Clerical Life* (1858), Dinah Morris in *Adam Bede* (1859), and Nicholas Bulstrode in *Middlemarch* (1872). The earlier portraits are very positive, but in Bulstrode she presents a serious critical consideration of what the Evangelical school represents.

▶ How strongly has religion been present as a theme in any Victorian novels you have read? Can you identify any specifically Evangelical attitudes or characteristics in these novels?

Bulstrode is not popular in Middlemarch – he is much too holier-than-thou for that ('To point out other people's errors was a duty that Mr Bulstrode rarely shrank from', and his 'tyrannical spirit, wanting to play banker and bishop everywhere' is remarked on). But Bulstrode is not a greedy, dominating hypocrite, as no doubt

Dickens would have presented him: one of his ongoing difficulties is how to live with himself, knowing what he knows about his own conduct.

So he leads a double life, outwardly a respectable, successful banker, a pillar of the church and the community, who had once had thoughts of a vocation in the Nonconformist ministry ('having had striking experience in conviction of sin and sense of pardon'). He married his employer's widow years before and, considerably enriched on her death, has subsequently married again, and is now 'a banker, a churchman, and a public benefactor'. But his inner life is one only he knows about, and is based on his knowledge of himself. His financial success, in fact, is based on a shabby act – not illegal, but contemptible; and the thought of losing the good opinion of society, his family, and most of all himself, if this should ever be known, is an agony to him. He is caught in a trap of his own past, and there is no solution to his dilemma:

> There were hours in which Bulstrode felt that his action was unrighteous: but how could he go back? He had mental exercises, called himself naught, laid hold on redemption, and went on his course of instrumentality.

And this is his other life. It is a masterly portrait of the contradictions and dilemmas which Evangelicalism could throw up.

The Evangelical clergy

The Evangelical clergy of the Church of England get a bad press in the Victorian novel: Jane Eyre's tormentor at Lowood, Mr Brocklehurst, is an example, and Trollope's Obadiah Slope in *Barchester Towers* (1857) is another. Slope, as near to the **dissenters** (members of the Nonconformist churches such as the Methodists, Baptists or Unitarians) in opinion as is possible in the Established Church, acts most powerfully on ladies with any 'spark of low church susceptibility', and uses them unscrupulously for his own ends. In *The Way of All Flesh* (1903), Samuel Butler's rueful retrospective view of Victorianism, Theobald Pontifex, Ernest's clerical father, represents all the pressures associated with Evangelicalism which poison Ernest's loveless childhood.

The Victorian Sunday

Another feature much associated with the Evangelical school, though it is not its exclusive property, is the Victorian Sunday, the day with '... nothing for the spent toiler to do, but to compare the monotony of his seventh day with the monotony of his six days, think what a weary life he led, and make the best of it ...'(*Little Dorrit*). Mr Slope, in *Barchester Towers*, makes a 'hobby' of 'Sunday observances': 'the "desecration of the Sabbath", as he delights to call it, is meat and drink to him'. For 'to him the revelation of God appears only in that one law given for Jewish observance', which is his chance to exercise dominion 'over at least a seventh part of man's allotted time here below'.

One famous description of the monotony, restriction and misery of a Victorian Sunday is in *Little Dorrit*, in Arthur Clennam's gloomy recalling of the 'dreary Sunday' of his childhood, 'the sleepy Sunday' of his boyhood, 'the interminable Sunday' of his adolescence, and 'the resentful Sunday' of his early manhood, when he returns from twenty years in China to find that nothing has changed. When he returns to London he encounters the same

> ... [m]elancholy streets, in a penitential garb of soot [which] steeped the souls of the people who were condemned to look at them out of windows, in dire despondency. ... Everything was bolted and barred that could by possibility furnish relief to an overworked people.

Outside commentators noted the same repression: in this time of 'grinding, pitiless, endless overwork which oppresses our nation like a spell ... holidays and Sundays we have ... but how joyless, stiff they are' (lecture by Frederic Harrison, 1867). The joyless Sunday is seen by the novelists (Dickens is not the only one: similar Sundays are memorably described in, for example, Mark Rutherford's *Autobiography* [1881] and in the pages of George Gissing's novels) as an image for a sick society so obsessed with materialism and its short-term rewards that it was oblivious of the true objects of life – 'happiness, refinement, education, health, civilisation itself' (Frederic Harrison, 1867).

▶ How does Dickens make his own attitude apparent through his writing? Look carefully at the diction (choice of vocabulary), alliteration and narrative point-of-view in the lines from *Little Dorrit* quoted above.

The Oxford Movement

If the Evangelical school represents one very significant area of Victorian religion which offered abundant material for the novelist, there were others. In the 1830s there was a fierce reaction among some clergy against what was seen as the growing secularisation of society, especially the tendency of politicians to regard the church as part of the state. A group of men at Oxford, notably J.H. Newman, John Keble and Edward Pusey, launched a series of tracts (religious pamphlets) in 1833 – hence the name, **Tractarians** – to remind the Church of England of the Catholic as well as Protestant aspects of its tradition. They stressed the Catholic side of Anglicanism, the place of sacraments in the church and other signs that the

Church of England was part of the universal church. The Oxford Movement led to a great revival of church life in the Anglican Church, and a great increase in the care and reverence with which its services were carried out. This in turn later brought about (though never under the direction of its early leaders) an appreciation of ritual and ceremonial.

Just as the leaders of the Evangelical school saw much to admire in the zeal for the scriptures found among Nonconformist churches, so the Oxford Movement, determined to preserve the Catholic as well as the Protestant sides of Anglicanism, could see much to admire in the Church of Rome that was part of the heritage of Anglicans as well as Roman Catholics. As some Evangelicals, finding the church indifferent to their urge for a new life, finally broke away and founded the Methodist Church, so Newman and others, despairing of influencing the Church of England, and fearing that it would become just a Protestant sect or department of state, left it for Rome.

The Oxford Movement and the novel

The furore in the church created by the tides of feeling surrounding these events had long lasting effects on society, and left its mark on the novel. Newman's conversion in 1845 was one famous example, and another more than twenty years later was that of the Marquess of Bute, who at twenty-one abandoned the Presbyterian Church of his Scottish upbringing for the Church of Rome. Both are recorded in fiction of the time.

Newman wrote his own fictional narrative of his conversion in *Loss and Gain* (1848), a powerful, passionate account of the young Charles Reding's voyage of discovery as his salvation in the Catholic Church becomes clear to him. Disraeli's novel *Lothair* (1870), in which the fight by the Catholic Church for the soul of a young aristocrat is a central theme, is based on the real-life episode in 1868 when the Roman Church claimed one of the premier nobles of Britain. Both novels sparkle with energy and wit, and are very readable accounts of a young man's mental journey, as well as of how the rumblings in the church were being felt in society. (There is an extract from *Loss and Gain* on pages 72–74.)

As the effects of Tractarianism began to pervade the community, the ideas behind the movement became the stuff of fiction. Aubrey St Lys in *Sybil* (1845) had been Disraeli's sympathetic portrayal of a High Church young priest. Trollope's Mr Arabin in *Barchester Towers* (1857) is a more penetrating picture of the beneficent effects of the Oxford Movement. Mr Arabin has come under the spell of Newman at Oxford, but has resisted the lure of Rome, though the magnetism of Newman's personality is still a powerful force with him. He is what the Tractarians have made him, but now:

He was content to be a high churchman, if he could be so on principles of his own, and could strike out a course showing a marked difference from those with whom he consorted.

Dickens, on the other hand, caricatures with relish the excesses of the Oxford Movement. Mrs Jellyby in *Bleak House* is obsessed with the missions (another Tractarian activity) and can 'see nothing nearer than Borrioboola Gha', though her own family is scandalously neglected. Mrs Pardiggle in the same novel is determined to improve society on Tractarian lines with or without their consent by her 'rapacious benevolence', and forces her reluctant young family, 'ferocious with discontent', to accompany her on every errand, including attendance at 'Mattins ... (very prettily done), at half-past six in the morning all the year round, including, of course, the depth of winter'.

The Heir of Redclyffe

Without question, the best-known novelist to write in the wake of the Oxford Movement is Charlotte Yonge. Brought up under the guidance of John Keble, the man who initiated the movement, she wrote novel after novel to promote the implicit teaching of the Tractarians. These novels are written with the reserve about religious things enjoined by the movement – she is silent about dogma and doctrine. Through plot and characterisation, she demonstrates the trials of attaining a holy life, and the difficulties attendant on genuine piety. This is not to suggest that the novels are boring, even to today's secular readers: the religion is almost entirely implied, and the interest resides in the skilful manipulation of character, realised in plot and dialogue.

Her most famous novel, *The Heir of Redclyffe*, has rarely been out of print since it was published in 1853. It concerns the struggle of the young hero, Sir Guy Morville, to master his powerful, impulsive temper, and how he conquers his doom with repentance, humility, and self-discipline. But the heir of the title is not, in fact, Guy (who inherits the baronetcy in the first chapter), but his cousin, Philip Edmonstone, and the story is as much of Philip's conquest over himself as it is of Guy's. Philip – overbearing, conceited, self-satisfied, and Guy's personal enemy – is a thoroughly disagreeable character. But at the end he is reduced to humble submissiveness, holding himself responsible for the death of Guy, whose title he inherits. There is no preaching at all in the novel, but the Tractarian details are there: Guy's veneration for Charles 1, his involvement with the foundation of a Tractarian sisterhood, his punctilious observance of services and sacraments are all identifying features of what came to be known as the **Anglo-Catholic Church**.

The novel was one of the most popular of the 19th century, and Guy was the role model for countless young Victorians – Burne-Jones and William Morris, the young Pre-Raphaelites, among them. Henry James, the American novelist, called Charlotte Yonge 'almost a genius',and the book is one of the most notable religious novels of the century.

Unbelief and doubt

The Victorian age may have been the most religious in history, but it was also the time when religion was most seriously questioned, and the word 'agnostic' was coined. Though 'infidelity' (in the sense of lack of Christian faith) was no new thing, its growth and spread, apparently throughout society, gave the middle classes much cause for unease – they associated atheism with the political instability of France and the violence there since the revolution of 1789, and were all the more frightened to detect signs of it in their own ranks.

There were various sources for the 'doubt': the 'Higher Criticism' of the Bible, which, in the light of new information, challenged the literal truth of Holy Writ, was one of the most significant causes. Much of the dangerous new knowledge was coming out of Germany: David Strauss, for example, had written *Das Leben Jesu (The Life of Christ)* in 1835, which George Eliot translated into English in 1846. Another was the growth of sciences like geology and biology. Darwin was the most notorious of the scientists, but he had been preceded by several others, and even his evolutionary theory (*The Origin of Species*, 1859) had been anticipated by his grandfather, Erasmus Darwin, and a French scientist, Lamarck.

To begin with the unbeliever was regarded by the general public with fear, as a subverter of society. In the earlier part of the period he (rarely she) was presented in the novel as a morally weak deviant. As the period went on, and doubt continued to pervade society, unbelief could no longer be put down simply to individual weakness, and the doubter began to be seen more as a victim, to be rescued and cured sooner than anathematised. By the end of the century he was often seen as a martyr, willing (for the sake of his conscience) to risk losing all advancement and even his place in society.

Doubt and the novel: *North and South* and *Robert Elsmere*

Mr Hale, in Elizabeth Gaskell's *North and South* (1855), is no villain: he is racked by doubt not about religion itself – 'No, not doubts as to religion: not the slightest injury to that' – but about some Anglican formularies to which the church requires him, as a priest, to assent. (These are left unspecified; but this was the time when the church was tearing itself asunder over matters of doctrine like baptismal regeneration and eternal damnation, over which many clergymen were unhappy.) In the circumstances he feels obliged to renounce his orders ('I must no longer be a minister in the Church of England') and to leave his comfortable south-country vicarage and seek secular employment as a private tutor in the industrial town of Milton-Northern.

Probably the most famous of all 'novels of doubt' is Mrs Humphry Ward's *Robert Elsmere* (1888), one of the best-sellers of the century, which swept through Britain and America like wildfire. (There is an extract on pages 84–85.) The Prime Minister Gladstone, himself a devout High Churchman, reviewed it seriously in the *Nineteenth Century*, calling it 'eminently an offspring of its time', and predicting that it would make a deep impression not only 'among mere novel-readers, but among those who share, in whatever sense, the deeper thoughts of the period'. Mrs Humphry Ward, the niece of Matthew Arnold, had plenty of experience of 'the deeper thoughts of the period', for her father Thomas Arnold was twice converted to the Roman Church, and she grew up in regions as far apart as Oxford, the Lake District, and Australia, where her father's changes in belief and thus profession took his family. She was no stranger to the turmoil that resulted for a family torn apart by religious difference.

Her most famous novel concerns just such a clash. Robert Elsmere, at Oxford when the influence of Newman was reviving in the 1870s, has had no problems with the theories of Darwin and the scientists, and has become a country parson, married to Catherine Leyburn, a devout and rigid Evangelical – 'the Thirty-Nine articles in the flesh', according to one rueful view. But Robert is scholarly by nature, and one of his parishioners is the atheistical, learned squire Roger Wendover, who is engaged on a massive *History of Testimony*, a study of all the sources on which Christianity depends – for thirty years he has been 'sifting and comparing the whole mass of existing records'. Wendover wishes to destroy Elsmere's faith with what he sees as evidence that Christ was the teacher, the martyr, but not the 'man-God, the Word from Eternity', and he succeeds. Robert's conscience will not allow him to continue as a hypocrite and he resigns his living: having rendered himself and his loving wife wretchedly unhappy and brought the marriage under severe strain, he moves to London. Here, he embarks on social work, and founds the 'New Brotherhood', a church based on 'Eternal Goodness – and an Eternal Mind – of which Nature and Man are the continuous and only revelation'. But for Robert 'the parting with the Christian mythology' has been 'the rending asunder of bones and marrow', and nowhere in Victorian literature is there a more poignant account of what it was like to lose one's faith.

The Empire

The theme of Empire is so pervasive in the Victorian novel, even when the central topic is not overtly colonial, that the reader is often barely conscious of its presence. But, though 'the Empire' is obvious in texts by novelists like Kipling, Rider

Haggard and Conrad, in fact in novel after novel throughout the period, it is possible to discern the political agenda which the Victorians took as much for granted as the Bank of England. With an unprecedented surge in empire building, British colonialism expanded during the Queen's reign to the point where Britain ruled the largest Empire the world had ever seen.

The impulse was trade, but although commerce and the making of money were central factors, the Empire was also largely won, governed, and administered by the younger sons of the middle classes. Indeed many families of all classes had members who made their careers overseas. Material of the Empire naturally found its place in the novel, and much of the fiction of Captain Marryat (1792–1848), R.M. Ballantyne (1825–1894), and G.A. Henty (1832–1902) promotes imperialist ideals. Towards the end of the century, Queen Victoria celebrated first her Golden Jubilee (1887) and ten years later her Diamond Jubilee, occasions which drew subjects from every part of the globe to London to commemorate her reign. 'The Empire' was headlines and the imperial theme became prominent in fiction. Much of the work of Rudyard Kipling (1865–1936) and Sir Henry Rider Haggard (1856–1925) celebrated it.

The Empire and the novel

Rider Haggard's *King Solomon's Mines* (1885), *She* (1887) and *Allan Quartermain* (1887) are extravagant novels of adventure which catch the mood of **jingoistic** ruthlessness that characterised contemporary colonialism. Rider Haggard himself was secretary to the Governor of Natal as a young man, and his descriptions of colonial exploitation are based on first-hand participation in episodes such as the British annexation of the Transvaal in 1887.

Rudyard Kipling's best-known novel is *Kim* (1901). Set in Imperial India, it is the story of the orphaned son of an Irish army sergeant, who is brought up in his father's regiment in Lahore, and becomes skilled in espionage. Through the eyes of Kim and his teachers, the old lama from Tibet and the native agent, Hurree Babu, the English reader becomes familiar with Kipling's India, the land of his birth and 'the jewel in the crown' of the British Empire.

From India, Kipling had been sent home to the Imperial Services College at Westward Ho!, Devon, a school where boys were trained for armed service in the Empire, and where he later set his novel *Stalky and Co.* (1899), a story of schoolboys preparing for this life. All the qualities and ideals required in the defence and administration of the Empire are fostered there – fervent nationalism, unswerving loyalty, unquestioning obedience (though always expressed with Kipling's humorous scepticism) – and boys are sent thence, via military training at Sandhurst or Woolwich, to fight as officers in frontier wars in Africa and Afghanistan.

Joseph Conrad (1857–1924) gives a rather different picture of the politics of colonialism in *Heart of Darkness* (1902), and his representation of the colonial enterprise in central Africa is devastating. The story was based on his own experience of a journey to the Congo to which he added, he says, 'a sinister resonance'.

But it is not only in central texts like these that readers today find the discourse of British colonialism. It is there as a necessary part of the background in a significant proportion of Victorian fiction. The East India Company, and other world trading centres, and British occupation in the east, for example, make a notable contribution to what the reader needs to know in *Vanity Fair* (Jos Sedley), in Elizabeth Gaskell's *Cranford* (1853) (Miss Matty's long-lost brother, Peter), and in *Little Dorrit* (the firm of Clennam and Son). Australia, the penal colony, is the source of Pip's great expectations, and then the subsequent site of his prosperity, while in *David Copperfield*, Little Em'ly and Mr Peggotty find a final safe haven there, and Mr Micawber prospers as a colonial magistrate. Emigration to the virgin plains and forests of Canada is the solution embraced by Mary and Jem in *Mary Barton* (and many other characters in other novels), and the mission-field offers a colonial setting to various novelists, for various motives.

For Charlotte Yonge, Canada, South Africa and the Pacific Islands are favourite destinations for those she sends to take the Word of God to the heathen (in *Hopes and Fears*, *New Ground*, *The Daisy Chain*, etc.). Dickens, satirising the whole missionary ideology, tells his readers that the feckless Mrs Jellyby in *Bleak House*, neglecting her family, can 'see nothing nearer than Africa'. Trollope, in similar vein, describes the missionary meeting in Barchester addressed by a fund-raiser for Sarawak, New Guinea and the Solomon Islands: after two days of harassment the whole of Barchester is glad to regard the whole subject 'as having been killed and buried' (*Framley Parsonage*).

Charlotte Brontë is equally ambivalent when she sends St John Rivers to die in the mission-field in *Jane Eyre*, though her most notable colonial contribution in the novel is the sinister part the West Indies plays in the lives of Jane and Mr Rochester as a result of his marriage to the Creole, Bertha Mason.

▶ How far do issues such as religion and colonialism play an explicit or implicit part in the Victorian novels you have read? In what ways might 21st-century attitudes towards Britain's colonial past lead you to rethink your attitude towards a character such as Rochester in *Jane Eyre* and towards Charlotte Brontë herself as novelist?

Politics

For much of the century parliamentary reform was a key issue in the national mind as the House of Commons, like so many other institutions, was restructured and reorganised. No fewer than four Reform Bills were passed between 1832 and 1918, and ancient procedures and conventions were abolished or reformed.

The political novel

The political scene had always been a rich source of material for the novel (one episode in *The Pickwick Papers* [1836–1837] concerns the parliamentary election at Eatanswill, when the Honourable Mr Samuel Slumkey, who makes the most of all the corrupt practices associated with an unreformed parliament, and is finally returned for the Blues), but as the reforming spirit gathered impetus in the context of the Second Reform Bill (1867), politics assumes a steadily more important position in the contemporary novel.

Trollope, turning from his earlier theme of the interpenetration of property and established religion in the 'Barsetshire' novels, switched in the 1860s and 1870s to the theme of the 'Palliser' novels, the interpenetration of property and politics. In novels like *Can You Forgive Her?* (1864), *Phineas Finn* (1869), *The Eustace Diamonds* (1873) and *The Prime Minister* (1876), Trollope shrewdly observes the compromises and half-measures that defeat political principle. In *The Way We Live Now* (1875), the election of the villain Melmotte to the safe Conservative seat of Westminster is a key episode in Trollope's bitterest novel (Melmotte's victory is due to the new Ballot Act of 1872, which made voting secret, and which Trollope deplored, feeling that it would lead to the election of candidates like Melmotte).

The election after the First Reform Bill of 1832 plays a part in George Eliot's *Middlemarch*. The candidate here is Mr Brooke, who is 'caught in political currents' which are coursing through society, but finds during his unhappy experience canvassing that time has moved on, and Middlemarch is not the cosy, paternalistic society he had imagined it: 'The weavers and tanners of Middlemarch ... had never thought of Mr Brooke as a neighbour, and were not more attached to him than if he had been sent in a box from London'. He is humiliatingly defeated in the election by the new electorate, which is assuming a new dispensation. (A contemporary critic called the whole novel 'a pent-up outcry against society', *Quarterly Review*, 1873.)

Probably the most overtly political novel, in that it deals directly with some of the political ideas of the 1860s, is George Eliot's *Felix Holt the Radical* (1866). Though set in 1832 and taking as its topic an election based on the results of the First Reform Bill, the novel was actually published in the run-up to the Second Reform Bill, and illustrates in fiction the issues surrounding this, in many ways, more momentous legislation. George Eliot, speaking through the **persona** of Felix Holt, a humble young artisan, urges the newly enfranchised electorate of working people that their hope of improvement lies not in this or that legislative programme, but in education. (She subsequently published an article, 'Felix Holt's Address to Working Men', purporting to be written by her mouthpiece, in which she spells this message out even more directly. There is an extract from the article in Part 3, pages 81–82.) This is Felix Holt's definition of 'radicalism'. He wishes to reform society from the bottom, and to see a redistribution of power – but not necessarily through votes:

> 'It's another sort of power that I want us working men to have, and I can see plainly enough that our all having votes will do little towards it at present ... I should like to convince you that votes would never give you political power worth having while things are as they are now, and that if you go the right way to work you may get power sooner without votes.'

Felix Holt does not, of course, have the property qualification required either to vote or to be an M.P., but George Eliot contrasts his views with those of the official Radical candidate, Harold Transome, whose political convictions do not rise above the parliamentary corruption of the day. Harold, who comes from the traditional Tory ruling class, has called himself 'a Radical only in rooting out abuses', but in fact 'disliked impracticable notions of loftiness and purity'. Felix Holt's radicalism is altogether more profound, and lies in his conviction that individuals must be changed before society can be reformed – and this cannot be effected by Parliament. Another high-minded young Radical, more obviously from the same Tory background as Harold, is Neil Beauchamp, who fights an unsuccessful election in George Meredith's *Beauchamp's Career* (1876).

The analysis of society

The Victorian novel, especially in the middle decades of the century, often has a documentary function and a historic significance quite outside any intrinsic merit as a work of art, though often enough the two features coincide. In the twenty years which followed the mid-century, there appeared a handful of novels which are great by any standards, and which provide a bird's-eye view of a whole society. None of them offers a close-up of any individual issue, but instead a panoramic view in which society at large is surveyed and its values assessed.

Hard Times

Hard Times (1854) is rather different from the other novels, and different from anything else that Dickens wrote. It is hardly a novel at all, in a conventional sense – the plot is of the thinnest, and there is no central character round whom the theme can be constructed. Dickens' memorable characters are really diagrammatic forms, cartoon figures which represent ideas, labelled with appropriate names. His target is the whole philosophy of industrialism rather than any specific industrial abuse, and is simultaneously a bitter attack on Utilitarianism. The tone is struck in the opening paragraphs, in the 'plain, bare monotonous vault of a schoolroom' as Mr Gradgrind declares to Mr M'Choakumchild and his pupils:

> Now, what I want is, Facts. Teach these boys and girls nothing but Facts. Plant nothing else, and root out everything else ... You are to be in all things regulated and governed ... by Fact. We hope to have, before long, a board of fact, composed of commissioners of fact, who will force the people to be a people of fact, and of nothing but fact ...

A central chapter of the novel, 'The Key-Note', continues the theme in the description of Coketown, the locale of the novel, as 'a triumph of fact ... everything was fact between the lying-in hospital and the cemetery ...'.

But against the image of Coketown, the 'town of machinery and tall chimneys', Dickens sets the image of Sleary's circus, which defies the System represented by Gradgrind and his partner Bounderby, and offers an alternative – a free life which values individuals, and urges the importance of spontaneity and imagination. This is where genuine feeling and an acknowledgement of relationships – the 'ology' which Mrs Gradgrind dies still looking for – are to be found:

> 'You learnt a great deal, Louisa, ... ologies of all kinds from morning to night. If there is any Ology left, of any description, that has not been worn to rags in this house, all I can say is, I hope I shall never hear its name ... But there is something – not an Ology at all, that your father has missed, or forgotten ... I shall never get its name now ...'

There are two longer extracts from *Hard Times* on pages 75–77.

Little Dorrit

Little Dorrit (1857), the novel which followed *Hard Times*, is Dickens' darkest view of contemporary society, and his most savage indictment of a materialistic age. In it he lashes the greed and hypocrisy masked by the Utilitarian ethic, and the abuses of privilege apparent in government (the topical issue which had ignited the fuse was the appalling mismanagement by the government of the **Crimean War**, 1854–1856). Every image in the novel is of decay, oppression, gloom, disease and death, and the central theme is of imprisonment.

The prisons range from the criminal gaol in Marseilles at the opening of the novel, and the 'quarantine barracks' in the same city where several of the principal characters are temporarily 'imprisoned', to the convent at the Great St Bernard Pass, and the Marshalsea Prison in London. And a central 'prison' is the 'old brick house, so dingy as to be all but black' near Cheapside where Mrs Clennam is imprisoned by her failing limbs, and which holds the innermost cell, her bedchamber. Arthur Clennam, back from his own imprisonment in the family firm in China, returns to the family home of parents who 'weighed, measured, and priced everything; for whom what could not be weighed and measured, and priced, had no existence', to be told by his mother 'The world has narrowed to these dimensions, Arthur ... I never leave my room.' From Pancks and the Plornishes, imprisoned in Bleeding Heart Yard, to the wealthy Merdle family imprisoned in Harley Street, every part of society is victim to constricting forces; even the nominally free are in fact confined.

Places, institutions, classes, families and individuals thus combine to create a picture of England as one huge prison with a multitude of cells. Dickens uses the prison metaphor ironically as he questions the whole concept of freedom: when Mr Dorrit is released from the Marshalsea, he takes the jail and his jailers with him to the outside world. Like his son, Tip, he appears 'to take the prison-walls with him' and to be 'of the prison prisonous'; with the stroke he suffers at the grand Merdle dinner party he reverts to the only reality he knows – imprisonment. Freedom, in fact, is a state of mind, and few characters in *Little Dorrit* enjoy it. Even Mr Merdle, the financier who rules the city and (apparently) enjoys unmeasured wealth, is always 'taking himself into custody under both coat-sleeves', and lives in his own private prison – and 'the name of Merdle is the name of the age'.

Little Dorrit is a very pessimistic novel. Dickens sets the forces of repression symbolically in the rapidly developing urban and industrial world where, it seemed to him, the selfish economic ethos which prevailed was actually threatening the human spirit, and he considers the full meaning of imprisonment. Nor does the novel suggest a solution or a release from these pressures, for in the final chapter the marriage of Arthur and Amy Dorrit resolves nothing – nothing is changed:

> They went quietly down into the roaring streets, inseparable and blessed; and as they passed along in sunshine and shade, the noisy and the eager, and the arrogant and the forward and the vain, fretted and chafed, and made their usual uproar.

▶ How does the picture of Victorian society presented by Dickens in *Little Dorrit* compare with your own images and ideas of England in the 19th century? Where have these images and ideas come from – history, books, architecture, paintings?

In *Hard Times* Dickens had created the vitality of Sleary's circus as an alternative to the dehumanising Gradgrind System of Coketown, and had suggested that the individual qualities of personal kindness, sympathy, honesty and warmth can and must be set against the deadening Utilitarian system. Elizabeth Gaskell, too, had in a similar way insisted that communication and sympathetic understanding between the classes would go far to alleviate the hardship that followed industrialisation. But there is no solution offered in *Little Dorrit*.

The Way We Live Now

The Way We Live Now (1875), one of Trollope's last novels, has moved on a long way from *The Warden* and *Barchester Towers* (1855, 1857): these are set in a time of what the author sees as fixed values, with a stable social order centred on a rural way of life. Twenty years later, however, Trollope is showing a mounting disquiet about the social, political, and moral well-being of the nation, and this disquiet is expressed in its most concentrated form in *The Way We Live Now*. The novel focuses on the story of the Carbury family, largely on Lady Carbury, her worthless son Sir Felix, and Roger Carbury, the head of the family, who is Trollope's embodiment of the traditional values of the past. But the real theme focuses on another Merdle-like figure, the shady financier, Melmotte. His great dinner, his election to Parliament, and his suicide are three cardinal events of the novel.

Trollope wrote in his *Autobiography* that he began *The Way We Live Now* to demonstrate 'what I conceived to be the commercial profligacy of the age', and he justified his indignation by describing '... a certain class of dishonesty, dishonesty magnificent in its proportions, and climbing into high places', which 'has become so rampant and so splendid ... men and women will be taught to feel that dishonesty, if it can become splendid, will cease to be abominable'. He declared that he would uncover not only 'the iniquities of the great speculator who robs everybody', but various other vices of contemporary society too.

Trollope shows every institution of society as seduced and compromised by Melmotte's millions – the aristocracy, the city, Parliament, the church. The lust for money is corrupting the nation from top to bottom, and the man who controls it wields ultimate power. The reputation for money ensures that Melmotte becomes the 'great man' of the day: 'the very navel of the commercial enterprise of the world'; the Member of Parliament for Westminster; host to the Royal Family and to the 'brother of the sun', the Emperor of China. '[S]uch a man', one character rhapsodises, 'rises above honesty as a general rises above humanity when he sacrifices an army to conquer a nation'. Yet Melmotte, as early as Chapter 4, has been described as of 'unpleasant' and 'untrustworthy' appearance, and with the look of 'the most gigantic swindler that ever lived'. Predictably his financial empire crashes around him, and he seeks the final solution (as had Merdle in *Little Dorrit*) in suicide – 'he was able to deliver himself from the indignities and penalties to which the law might have subjected him by a dose of prussic acid'.

Melmotte is the rotten centre of *The Way We Live Now*, but in his orbit are representatives of the whole degenerate society. Sir Felix Carbury is a dissolute young baronet, who has already run through the inheritance left by his father, and has one intention in life – to maintain his accustomed lifestyle in the Guards and his aptly-named club, the Beargarden, by any means, however dishonourable. Marriage to Melmotte's daughter would ensure the means. His friends – effete young aristocrats like Miles Grendall and Dolly Longstaffe – and their families and circle are similar, and are prepared to sell themselves for what they can get from Melmotte.

One character resists the meretricious lure of Melmotte: Roger Carbury, the head of the family and a Suffolk country squire, is Trollope's representative of the old order, and speaks with Trollope's voice. But in this urban world of commercial speculation the gentry and aristocracy are compromised, and Roger Carbury is virtually penniless: his values, however vigorously he defends them, belong to the past, in a feudal society – and as he remains a bachelor to the end, the implication is that they will die with him.

The intellectual novel

In the 1870s the novel entered a new phase, and with the deaths of George Eliot in 1880 and Trollope in 1882 it could almost be said that the 'Victorian novel' came to an end. In the earlier years of the Queen's reign, the emphasis in the novel had been on social orientation and the adjustment of the individual to society, with stress on character. There had followed novels which were indictments of society as a whole. The novels of the 1870s and 1880s were philosophically probing, more symbolic, more poetic than before, and this period saw the emergence of novelists like Hardy, Conrad and Henry James. The decades overlap, of course, and no dates can be confidently applied; but trends become obvious and generalisations possible.

The intellectual, psychological emphasis of the novel was becoming perceptible in the later work of George Eliot. In *Middlemarch* (1871–1872) Eliot offers a whole study of provincial life, largely through an analysis of the personalities which make it up: in the relationships between them, and in the social, personal and professional interaction of the characters, she shows how petty jealousies and conflicts, both major and minor, make up the moral texture of society.

Middlemarch

In one sense *Middlemarch* is another indictment of a society which denies scope to the intellect and obstructs the remarkable, but the tone never has the sombre quality of Dickens or the bitterness of Trollope. There is no single figure like Melmotte, for society is collectively responsible for the spirit of compromise which rules. The integration of the individual with society is presented not as an achievement, but as a defeat of individual aspiration.

The obvious examples in *Middlemarch* are Dorothea Brooke and Lydgate. Dorothea, 'so substantive and rare a creature', whose 'mind was theoretic, and yearned by its nature after some lofty conception of the world ... [and] was enamoured of intensity and greatness and rash in embracing whatever seemed to her to have those aspects', ends by being 'absorbed into the life of another, and ... only known in a certain circle as a wife and mother'. Lydgate, who has come to Middlemarch as a young doctor determined to 'stage [his] own deeds and alter the world a little', and who is at first absorbed in an ambitious scientific investigation of the primitive tissue, concludes by writing 'a treatise on Gout, a disease which has a good deal of wealth on its side'.

Self-realisation rather than integration is the theme in the later Victorian novel, and the emphasis shifts from social behaviour to the inner life. Ideas are as important as characters and whole philosophies of life are examined. So, in *Middlemarch*, Lydgate, with his fashionable wife and comfortable income, has made a success of his life by the standards of earlier Victorian orthodoxy, but dies regarding himself as a failure – 'he had not done what he once meant to do'. Dorothea, too, has settled for the second-best. As a girl she acted 'as if she thought herself living in the time of the Apostles', and aspires to a way of life nobler than the Middlemarch way of life; but at the end of the novel, 'Dorothea could have liked nothing better, since wrongs existed, than that her husband should be in the thick of a struggle against them, and that she should give him wifely help'. They are both victims of society.

In *Middlemarch*, for the first time, fiction has become intellectual, concerned with ideas about the nature of the individual and society. Virginia Woolf, the 20th-century novelist, described it as 'one of the few English novels written for grown-up people'.

The Egoist

George Meredith was once regarded as highly as George Eliot, though his popularity has now waned. Sigmund Freud, the father of psychoanalysis, thought that Meredith was the most penetrating psychologist of all the English novelists, and Oscar Wilde declared that he was 'philosophy in fiction. His people not merely live, but they live in thought.' In his finest novel *The Egoist* (1879) the plot, such as it is, revolves around Sir Willoughby Patterne, an insufferably selfish and conceited baronet, and his relationship with the women he has selected as the potential partners of his life. There is as much pattern in the structure of the novel as in the name of the central character.

The selection Willoughby makes becomes something of a minuet as Meredith moves the pieces round: Laetitia Dale, '[Willoughby's] image of the constant woman', has been in love with him all her life, but, lacking birth and fortune, has always been in a weak position; Constantia Durham accepts him but quickly realises her mistake, jilts him, and elopes with an officer in the Hussars; Clara

Middleton, the 'dainty rogue in porcelain', is trapped after a whirlwind courtship, but is quickly repelled by his monstrous egoism ('in his hungry coveting to be loved more and still more, more still, until imagination gave up the ghost, he talked to her plain hearing like a monster'), and her liberation is the main strand of the story.

When Willoughby Patterne, the monomaniac whose self-love is threatened by the rejection of two women, eventually turns in desperation to Laetitia Dale, it is only to find that the scales have fallen from her eyes. 'I was a foolish romantic girl', she tells him, but 'now I am a sickly woman, all illusions vanished ... I am an Egoist.' By fierce talking Willoughby persuades Laetitia to accept him in spite of her misgivings, but on her terms. The pattern is complete when Clara Middleton marries Vernon Whitford, Willoughby's friend, but his opposite in every respect.

The Egoist is a novel of ideas in which Meredith played with the thoughts which were engrossing him. He had, for example, just written his major critical work, *An Essay on Comedy* (1877), and the subtitle of the novel is *A Comedy in Narrative*. The opening chapter is an essay examining the role of comedy in literature and in it Meredith formulates his theories on both. The central character calls to mind the 'willow pattern' of Chinese porcelain, the story of which depicts the flight of a hapless maiden from both tyrannical father and fiancé.

This is not to say that the intellectual novel is not entertaining: in *The Egoist* the sharp characterisation of Clara Middleton, the 'New Woman', and Crossjay Patterne, the engaging twelve-year-old, and the brilliance of the dialogue, are notable features of its material and presentation. These, and the vitality, wit and social satire, make the novel unforgettable.

Thomas Hardy

It is interesting to note at this point that both Meredith and Hardy thought of themselves primarily as poets, though it is as novelists that they are chiefly remembered today. Both, certainly, brought poetic techniques to fiction, and wrote using symbols and images rather than the details of every day. Hardy said more than once in his later novels, '... a novel is an impression, not an argument' (Preface, *Tess of the d'Urbervilles*), and '[it] is simply an endeavour to give shape and coherence to a series of seemings, or general impressions, the question of their consistency or their discordance ... being regarded as not of the first moment' (Preface, *Jude the Obscure*).

▶ How helpful do you find Hardy's anti-intellectual definitions as ways of thinking about the novel? Can any novels by other authors you have read be described as 'simply an endeavour to give shape and coherence to a series of seemings, or general impressions'?

Hardy, like Meredith, saw human life as presided over by cosmic forces which manipulate events. But while Meredith's spirits work in the end for harmony, and are positive forces, in Hardy the fates bring about what is already determined, and Hardy's view of what the 'President of the Immortals' intends is deeply pessimistic. He saw the individual as struggling in vain against the rigid codes of behaviour which governed society, and the late-Victorian world as caught up in a spiral of decay as the old rural ways were destroyed by industrial efficiency. In *The Mayor of Casterbridge* (1886) and *Tess of the d'Urbervilles* (1891) the conflict between the two sets of values, the old and the new, is at the root of the human tragedies of both novels.

Hardy's greatest novels belong to the group he called 'Novels of Character and Environment', and all concern the struggle of the individual with the hostile or, at best, indifferent forces of nature. This struggle is represented, for example, in *The Return of the Native* (1874) through the hopeless battle of the outsiders Eustacia Vye and Damon Wildeve against the sullen malignity of nature in the form of Egdon Heath; or in Giles Winterborne's battle with the rain and the wood in *The Woodlanders* (1887).

Blind Chance, or Hap, as Hardy called it, is also against humankind: through pure ill-luck, for instance, Mrs Yeobright fails to gain entrance to Clym's house and wanders away to her death on Egdon Heath (*Return of the Native*), and Tess's crucial letter to Angel Clare, pushed under the door, disappears under the mat and is lost.

But if the forces of nature, indifferent or hostile, and the workings of Fate combine to shape human destiny, the constrictions of Victorian convention (just as much part of the environment) are as powerful, and invariably malign. By the time of Hardy's late novels the 'Immanent Will', which has been seen increasingly to direct events, is joined as a hostile force by the strictures of society, which destroy the individual just as relentlessly as Fate and Nature do.

Tess of the d'Urbervilles

All these features – the poetic treatment of the novel, the changing nature of society, the malignity of fate, the pressures of society, the accidents and coincidences which doom the individual – come together most obviously in *Tess of the d'Urbervilles* (1891), perhaps the most poetic of all Hardy's novels. Here, Hardy concentrates in single characters what he saw as a whole way of life collapsing under the agricultural depression of the 1870s and 1880s. English prosperity was passing from rural to urban areas, and those who worked on the land were caught up inexorably in this downward slide. In *Tess* Hardy suggests that the conflict between the old rural ideologies and the oppression of modern efficiency is at the root of the human tragedies he portrays. Added to this is the yet more damaging source of human destruction – the despotic social code of behaviour imposed by Victorian convention.

Hardy's main purpose and conviction is defined by his thought-provoking sub-title, *A Pure Woman*. Tess is a fallen woman, a kept mistress, finally a murderer – and still, defiantly, a pure woman. For Hardy she is pure of heart, with all the gifts of humanity and compassion, the greatest virtues – and simply a victim of circumstances. The circumstances are accidents and coincidences, which militate against her and are the work of a malevolent Fate but also the result of Tess's inherited dreaminess. So, Prince the horse is spitted by the mail-cart and dies leaving the Durbeyfields penniless, Tess's letter of confession to Angel Clare miscarries fatally, Angel's parents are not at home when Tess visits the vicarage, and so on. There is probably more of the accidental in *Tess* than in any other Hardy novel, but in the world of *Tess* this is normality and part of the life-view which Hardy was using the novel to express.

Tess was not the first Victorian novel to treat of seduction and illegitimacy ('frankness' was a feature of the late-century novel), but it was the first to portray the victim so passionately as heroine – and Victorian puritanism was outraged. Hardy's themes, the inviolability of purity and the uncertainty of reputation, are the themes of poetry, and this is how Hardy treated them. Naturalistic detail, where it is used in *Tess*, has a metaphoric function, and social relations are seen against a symbolic natural background. The forces in Tess's life are represented, for example, by the locales and seasons in which she finds herself. In the summer, the time of her joy, she is in the idyllic Talbothays where

> … amid the oozing fatness and warm ferments of the Var Vale, at a season when the rush of juices could almost be heard below the hiss of fertilisation, it was impossible that the most fanciful love should not grow passionate …

and where 'Tess in her recent life had never been so happy as she was now'. Then, in the winter, when her life has changed, the scene shifts to the sombre wastes and flinty uplands of Flintcomb-Ash, the 'starve-acre place' of Tess's darkest time.

On another level, the **symbolism** of blood appears consistently and deliberately throughout the novel, from the death of Prince to the murder of Alec ('[T]he oblong white ceiling, with this scarlet blob in the midst, had the appearance of a gigantic ace of hearts'), to the sacrificial altar at Stonehenge, where Hardy lays Tess as an offering to the gods of Victorian propriety. Even the 'piece of blood-stained paper caught up from some meat-buyer's dust-heap', and the agonising death of the blood-stained wounded pheasants, play their part. As she gazes at the piteous condition of the birds, Tess reflects ruefully that her misery is caused not by physical pain or mutilation; it is the consequence of nothing more tangible than a sense of condemnation under 'an arbitrary law of society which had no foundation in Nature'. Hardy implicitly invites the reader to consider which is worse, the sufferings of the birds or the sufferings of Tess.

The implications of *Tess* are uncompromisingly tragic, and it is tragedy on an epic, universal scale. The final sentence brings to mind the greatest of all English epics, *Paradise Lost*, and the expulsion of Adam and Eve from Eden ('They hand in hand, with wandering steps and slow, / Through Eden took their solitary way'). At the end of Hardy's novel, Angel Clare and Lisa-Lu – 'a spiritualised image of Tess' – stand vigil on a hill overlooking the city of Wintoncester where Tess is executed ('"Justice" was done, and the President of the Immortals ... had finished his sport with Tess'); and then 'As soon as they had strength they arose, joined hands again, and went on'.

Victorian twilight

When the Victorian age drew to a close, the understanding of the nation, and its perception of itself, were very different from what they had been half a century before. The confidence that followed the Industrial Revolution and British economic supremacy in the middle decades of the century had been much checked by international competition in Europe and America, and there were tensions in the Empire, especially in South Africa. The **Boer Wars** between 1881 and 1902 had rocked confidence in the imperial idea, and in British military efficiency. The 'Victorian values' which had marked so much of the century were being questioned; and the novel reflects this dip in national morale.

Jude the Obscure

For the first time the theme of failure became a significant element in the novel, and nowhere more obviously than in Hardy (though George Gissing in, for example, *Born in Exile* [1892] and *The Odd Women* [1893] is another eminent example). Hardy's last novel, *Jude the Obscure* (1895), is the story of an unheroic victim of external forces who fails in every aspect of life, domestic, academic and professional, and dies murmuring 'Let the day perish wherein I was born ...'.

Jude's struggle against implacable fate accords him heroic stature of a sort, but in making the theme of the novel 'the contrast between the ideal life a man wished to lead and the squalid real life he was fated to lead' (Hardy, in a letter to a friend), the author stacked all the cards against Jude, who is a very human figure. His life is not tragic in any but the ancient Greek sense, for all that befalls him is predestined by 'blind Chance', and Jude is only a puppet to demonstrate issues in the author's mind. He wants 'to tell, without a mincing of words, of a deadly war waged ... between flesh and spirit; and to point the tragedy of unfulfilled aims ...' (Preface).

Nonetheless, it is Hardy's most devastating indictment of a system constrained by convention and tradition, and of a rural life vitiated by debased urban values. The novel is, in one sense, a parallel to *Tess*, in that the disaster in both springs largely from early sexual misfortunes – both central characters, Tess and Jude, are fated to fall in love with 'intellectuals' who are 'ethereal'. However, the likeness ends there, for Angel Clare turns out to be the embodiment of Victorian double standards, while Sue Bridehead is an advanced, emancipated girl of the time who views marriage with distrust and looks for sexual liberty. For Sue marriage is a trap, and she asks Jude urgently:

> 'Jude, do you think that when you must have me with you by law, we shall be as happy as we are now? ... Don't you dread the attitude that insensibly arises out of legal obligation? Don't you think it is destructive to a passion whose essence is its gratuitousness?'

Thus one tradition targeted by Hardy is marriage, which he condemns in terms of its social conventions. While Sue cries 'It is no good fighting against God!' as they enjoy an adulterous love, Jude puts it differently: 'It's only men and senseless circumstances.'

Hardy's other main target in *Jude the Obscure* is the inaccessibility of higher education for the working man. Jude's ambition is to study at Christminster (Oxford) and then to become a clergyman. But scholarship and sensuality, the one his aspiration, the other his undoing, are brought ludicrously together at the beginning of the novel: while he daydreams absently about learning and preferment he is 'smacked sharply in the ear' by 'the characteristic part of a barrow-pig' as Arabella attracts his attention with a pig's pizzle.

Arabella, a paradigm of sensuality, traps Jude into marriage, and then leaves him, indifferently, to pursue his earlier ambition. But he is as thwarted in his attempts to enter Christminster as in his doomed marriage: Christminster does not want to know him. The 'scholared walls' of the colleges – Cardinal, Rubric, Sarcophagus, Biblioll – remain 'silent, black, and windowless' and throw their 'four centuries of gloom, bigotry, and decay, shutting out the moonlight by night and the sun by day', and Jude remains 'an outsider to the end of his days'.

Little Father Time, Jude's son by Arabella, is the gruesome symbol in the novel of 'the growing wish not to live' and the mood of questioning self-doubt which marked the last years of the century. He commits suicide after killing his half-brothers and sisters and leaves a note explaining 'Done because we was too menny'.

Jude the Obscure is thus something of a companion piece to *Tess of the d'Urbervilles* in theme, but it is the more profound. In the earlier novel the drama, the emotion, the suffering are on a heroic scale; in the latter, even bleaker, version,

Jude puts his finger on the problem when he says 'We are horribly sensitive; that's what's the matter with us, Sue!' Where the final sport of the President of the Immortals is to see Tess, the last representative of the d'Urbervilles, hanged in Wintoncester Gaol, Jude wastes away with TB and dies miserable and alone in a Christminster back street. The later novel encapsulates the unease and self-doubt that marked the last years of the century – a mood echoed in Hardy's poetry, the medium in which he mainly wrote after *Jude the Obscure*.

The Way of All Flesh

'Victorian values' (as they are recorded in the Victorian novel) could be said to have come to an end abruptly when Samuel Butler wrote *The Way of All Flesh* in 1873. Butler worked on revisions of the novel intermittently throughout the decade, completed revision of it in the 1880s, but decided against publication until after his death – when, he supposed, the individuals to be identified in his swingeing attack on all things Victorian would also be dead. (The novel was published in 1903.) Prime among these were his parents, and behind them his headmaster and the other authority figures of his youth. When he had finished with them, little remained of the Victorian world which they personified, for Butler had smashed every Victorian icon of convention and respectability.

The novel is largely autobiographical. The central figure, Ernest Pontifex (Butler himself), grows up in a clerical family (Butler's father was Vicar of Langar, near Nottingham, and his grandfather was a famous bishop), and the Revd. Theobald Pontifex is based heavily on Butler's father, for whom he remembered no childhood feelings except fear and shrinking.

Butler deals a deathblow to the Victorian myth of parenthood and family life in his unsparing pictures of Theobald and Christina – and indeed of the previous Pontifex generation, for Ernest is not the first Pontifex victim: Theobald, forced by his father into a life for which he has no vocation, has acquired Christina as a prize in a game of cards –

> The next morning saw Theobald in his rooms coaching a pupil, and the Miss Allabys in the eldest Miss Allaby's bedroom playing at cards with Theobald for the stakes.

Theobald, the reluctant husband, loses no time at all in asserting the position of authority conferred on him in the marriage-service, and Christina is instantly obliged to become a loving and obedient wife. As a father, Theobald does not spare the rod. His relationship with Ernest, his eldest child, is that between Butler and his father, as the author recorded in a letter:

He never liked me, nor I him; from my earliest recollections I can call
to mind no time when I did not fear him and dislike him.

One famous episode, when Ernest is very small, illustrates Theobald's view of
fatherhood, and explains Ernest's later attitude to his father. Ernest has a lisp and
cannot say 'Come'; he succeeds only in saying 'Tum', which Theobald regards as
wilful and treats accordingly:

> We could hear screams coming from the dining-room ... and knew
> that Ernest was being beaten. 'I have sent him to bed', said Theobald,
> as he returned to the drawing-room, 'and now, Christina, I think we
> will have the servants in to prayers', and he rang the bell for them,
> red-handed as he was.

Christina is little better: where Theobald is violent and unreasonable, Christina is
treacherous and manipulative. 'Nevertheless,' the narrator tells us, 'she was fond of
her boy ... and it was long before she could destroy all affection for herself in the
mind of her first-born. But she persevered.'

As for the relationship between man and wife, expressed in the Victorian myth
of the sanctity of marriage and so damagingly exposed in the betrothal of the
Pontifexes, it is summed up in Theobald's behaviour at his wife's funeral:

> 'She has been the comfort and mainstay of my life for more than
> thirty years,' said Theobald, as soon as it was all over, 'but one could
> not wish it prolonged', and he buried his face in his handkerchief to
> conceal his want of emotion.

The myth of childhood and the Victorian family is exploded in a passage which
Butler finally deleted from Chapter 6, and which asks if any form of life could
possibly be 'so awful as childhood in a happy united God-fearing family'.

Father-figures as a whole get short shrift in *The Way of All Flesh*. Dr Skinner,
the headmaster of Roughborough School where Ernest is sent, emerges as
tyrannous, hypocritical and full of 'blundering and capricious cruelty'. Butler's
narrator describes him as always speaking in words which have 'a deeper and
hidden meaning' and then recalls the evening when Skinner's request for a supper
of 'a glass of cold water and a small piece of bread and butter' is subsequently
translated to 'a good plate of oysters, a scallop shell of minced veal, nicely browned,
some apple tart, and a hunk of bread and cheese', plus gin and hot water with
lemon. The quality of his mind 'might be perceived by the solemnity with which he
spoke even of trifles'.

Butler's irony is directed with deadly force against individuals who represent the sacred cows of Victorianism: he deals with parents and the family, and education, and moves to religion and the church when Ernest, destined for ordination, encounters models of the Evangelicals and the High Church – and finally with the free-thinkers, by whom he is readily defeated. Ernest moves with 'snipe-like flights' from one position to another as he learns to see what shams are concealed by conventional religion, and it is not until he unexpectedly finds himself in prison, the result of a misunderstanding with a lady, that the revelation comes:

> He knew he had been humbugged, and he knew also that the greater part of the ills which had afflicted him were due, indirectly, in chief measure to the influence of Christian teaching ...

For a time his intention is 'to convert the whole Church of England to free-thought ... Christianity would become extinct in England in a few months' time'. With the support of the 'kindly, sensible' chaplain, the most attractive Christian in the novel, Ernest emerges from prison a new man, on target to become (after sundry twists in the plot) the easy bachelor, in comfortable circumstances, amiably free from the constraints of Victorianism – in other words, Butler himself.

▶ How does Butler's narrator, in the extracts from *The Way of All Flesh* quoted above, make clear his contempt for the characters and their double standards?

Assignments

1. Margaret Thatcher, when Prime Minister (1978–1991), called for a return to 'Victorian values'. List those values that are held up for approval and and those that are put forward for condemnation in the novels you have studied.

2. Victorian novels often paint a vivid picture of life at different levels of society during the 19th century. Is it safe to assume that what you read represents an accurate picture? Can any novel ever produce a complete or unprejudiced picture?

3. Some of the novels discussed above have remained in print for over 150 years; others have gone out of fashion and out of print. Some have achieved the status of 'classics', others can be seen as interesting but less important or successful. Who makes these judgements? On what basis are they made? On what grounds would you yourself allow some works, but not others, to be part of the **canon** of Victorian fiction?

2 | Approaching the texts

- Why were novels so popular in Victorian England?

- What is meant by 'the author'?

- What is the relationship between author and reader?

- What are the conventions of a Victorian novel?

- How were Victorian novels published?

'A novel-reading people'

The novel was not, of course, invented by the Victorians, but it assumed a significance and importance for them that made this the age of the novel. Edmund Gosse, the writer and critic, was reflecting at the end of the century that 'the Victorian has been peculiarly the age of the triumph of fiction' (*National Review*, 1892). It had developed in the hands of Daniel Defoe (*Robinson Crusoe*), Laurence Sterne (*Tristram Shandy*), Samuel Richardson (*Pamela*) and Henry Fielding (*Tom Jones*), as a new art form, but by the start of the 19th century still had to establish itself: in critical terms the novel was accorded less prestige and status than the traditional forms of poetry. Even as late as the 1880s, Trollope could write 'By the common consent of all mankind who have read, poetry takes the highest place in literature' (*Autobiography*), but by the death of Queen Victoria in 1901, the novel had come to be recognised as 'the Victorian epic', the highest of all literary genres. And it enjoyed phenomenal popularity right through society. As Anthony Trollope observed more than once:

> We have become a novel-reading people, from the Prime Minister down to the last appointed scullery maid ... [All] our reading put together hardly amounts to what we read in novels.
> (Lecture in Edinburgh, 1870)

and

> Novels are read right and left, above stairs and below, in farm houses and country parsonages, by young countesses and by farmers' daughters, by old lawyers and by young students.
> (*Autobiography*)

What were the reasons for the spectacular success of the novel? One concern of fiction, of course, had always been entertainment, at least from the time of Sir Philip Sidney who wrote about the teller of a tale 'which holdeth children from play, and old men from the chimney corner' (*Defence of Poesie*, 1595). One purpose of the Victorian tale was no different: fiction was there to divert and to amuse.

This was where fiction's disparagers found most of their ammunition. To its detractors, fiction had no other function. It was associated exclusively with relaxation and entertainment, things against which women and the young must be warned and which, for men, was on a par with 'armchairs, pipes, and slippers' (*Fraser's Magazine*, 1879). Novel reading, and the habit of endless storytelling, 'it was felt, are hardly likely to encourage strenuous thought' (*Saturday Review*, 1873) and should therefore be discouraged. On even more openly moral grounds, a (diminishing) party in the church, mostly of the Evangelical school, viewed fiction as a form of lying, and denounced it vigorously.

At the same time, it had to be acknowledged – with alarm by its detractors – that the novel was quite phenomenally popular, at all levels and among all types of people. Darwin, Matthew Arnold and Cardinal Newman, for example, were all enthusiastic readers; Elizabeth Barrett Browning was a voracious consumer and the newly published titles would arrive monthly at her father's house, first in Herefordshire and then at Wimpole Street, and eventually were sent from England when she was living abroad.

But, particularly in the middle decades of the century, there were continuing voices raised against the potential dangers of the novel in corrupting women and the young, and against its fatal effects on the 'moral fibre' of the nation. It was a lingering prejudice against which the developing form had to contend, that fiction was only for entertainment and relaxation. In his autobiography, Trollope remembered that in his young days, in the 1820s, novel reading was often a forbidden luxury: 'families in which an unrestricted permission was given for the reading of novels were very few, and from many they were altogether banished'; and he recalled that even at the other end of the century, there was still sometimes a feeling that 'novels at their best are but innocent' – not serious literature, in fact. It was an 'embargo,' he said, which novelists found 'a much heavier tax than that of full want of full appreciation'.

The threat it posed to the morals of society was a prime element in the case against the legitimacy of the novel. In 1863 Wilkie Collins, himself a popular author, wrote a rueful indictment of the double standards of the reading public:

> If the dull people of our district were told tomorrow that my wife, daughters and nieces had all eloped in different directions, leaving just one point of the compass open as a runaway outlet for me and

the cook, I feel firmly persuaded that not one of them would be inclined to discredit the report: 'This is what comes of novel-reading!' they would say ...

(My Miscellanies)

On the other hand, one of the most important functions of the novel, as it was perceived by a great many of its readers, was instruction. In an age of bewildering change an increasingly literate society looked to the novel for guidance and direction. Through the imaginative depiction of other worlds and characters, the Victorian reader was given access to the reality of feelings and moral issues outside his/her individual experience. Novelists offered reassurance, and often took on the role of sage and mentor. As late as 1872, one periodical was discussing the 'high-minded and impartial authors of fiction, the brilliancy of whose writing is no less conspicuous than the purity of their moral teaching ... by this instrumentality education has been advanced, social abuse rectified, and virtue generally encouraged' (*Gentleman's Magazine*, 1872).

As early as the 1840s, serious reviews of new novels were appearing in the press, and occupied the same space as serious analyses of contemporary politics and culture. Among the more prestigious quarterlies and monthlies the *Westminster Review*, *Blackwood's*, the *Prospective* and *North British Review* all took fiction seriously, while *Fraser's Magazine* published the most interesting novel criticism.

The novelists themselves were very conscious of the responsibility of this position. Trollope wondered whether he and his colleagues had 'done good or evil to the people who read them,' and went on, 'I can assert that such thoughts have been strong with them and with myself' (*Autobiography*). George Eliot affirmed her own motives for writing:

The only effect I ardently long to produce by my writings is that those who read them should be better able to imagine and feel the pains and joys of those who differ from themselves in everything but the broad fact of being struggling, caring human creatures.

(Letter to Charles Bray, 1859)

The novelist, she said, is the 'teacher or influencer of the public mind'. For the public at large in an era before mass entertainment, the part played by the novelist and the novel in providing therapeutic relaxation was extremely important. They provided a form of escapism, in itself a psychological necessity in an era of chaotic change. In an age of what Arnold called 'doubts, disputes, distractions, fears', the novel made a significant contribution to what was going on in people's minds – it presented the actuality of choice in the different kinds of moral possibility, and gave an extension to consciousness.

So how was the novel to answer those who trivialised it as escapism? Throughout the century the novelist had been attacked intermittently for being a mere entertainer, for the undemanding motive of his/her work, for the lack of toughness of the novel as a genre; but in the last two decades of the century the intellectual prestige of the novel was established almost beyond dispute.

The 'intellectual' novel, where the intention was unquestionably more than amusement, had had its beginnings in George Eliot, and its position as the principal vehicle of thought and philosophy was confirmed by Meredith, Hardy and other novelists of the later years. George Eliot had prepared the way with novels like *Middlemarch* (1872) and *Daniel Deronda* (1876), and Meredith confirmed the intellectual eminence of the novel with *The Egoist* (1879). Those whose intention was to rescue the novel from its critics welcomed *The Egoist* on the grounds of its difficulty; and Meredith lent his weight, declaring that the novel should represent all that was cerebral rather than moral or entertaining.

Thomas Hardy, writing at the same time, was as serious as Meredith about the nature and function of fiction, and discussed his theories and ideas in his different Prefaces to, for example, *Tess of the d'Urbervilles*, *Jude The Obscure* and *The Woodlanders*. And in the novels of Henry James, written from the late 1870s onwards and perhaps the most 'intellectual' of all, could be seen the most decisive and obvious shift in emphasis from subject to form.

'Seriousness' was a defining feature of the novel in the last two decades of the century. The intellectual controversies raging in religious, scientific, and philosophical fields were the material of such best-sellers as Mrs Humphry Ward's *Robert Elsmere* (1888), J.H. Shorthouse's *John Inglesant* (1881) and Walter Pater's *Marius the Epicurean* (1885). Another successful function of the novel throughout the period, was the dissemination of information and opinion. 'There is, indeed,' remarked the *Westminster Review* in the early days, 'hardly a theory, an opinion, or a crotchet, which has not been given to the world in the three-volume form.'

Women novelists

When W.S. Gilbert gave Pooh Bah the little list in *The Mikado* (1885), it contained among the targets of his satire the Lady Novelist, for by then women who wrote had long been an accepted section of society and legitimate targets of (male) satire. The profession of novelist had always been open to women, from the time of Clara Reeve and Fanny Burney, Ann Radcliffe and Maria Edgeworth, in the early days of the novel. Jane Austen, with the wide public esteem she enjoyed from the beginning, confirmed the position of the woman novelist. True, George Eliot in a famous article in the middle of the century, 'Silly Novels by Lady Novelists', had appeared to equate women novelists with governesses, women who adopted the profession 'because they had no other lady-like means of getting their bread'; but she spoke merely of what she called the 'Mind – and – Millinery species,' who scribbled to avoid destitution. And her jibes did confirm that society accepted literary women as a genus. Literary women, in fact, were recognised both socially and professionally. In 1855 Margaret Oliphant, herself a prolific novelist, wrote an article in *Blackwood's Magazine* on 'Modern Novelists – Great and Small' in which she claimed that the emerging Victorian age 'which is the age of many things ... is quite as distinctly the age of female novelists'. Two-thirds of the novelists selected for review in *Blackwood's* were female.

▶ Are you aware of any differences in status or seriousness between male and female novelists today? Does the sex of a novelist (Victorian or contemporary) have any effect on the way you select, read or judge a novel?

With the burgeoning success of the novel from the 1830s onwards, the contribution of women to the **genre** came to be acknowledged as significant in defining the function and conventions of the new form. A reviewer in the *Westminster* in 1853 saw this phenomenon both as going back to the 18th century, and as assuming an additional role in the novel of his own time:

> As the last century approached its close, the change of manners once more marked itself strongly in the fictions of the time. Lady authors became more numerous ... [The] new school makes up for its inferiority in power and nature, by irreproachable modesty and propriety of tone. It was reserved for the present category to prove that both qualities could exist together.

Women were recognised now, moreover, as being quite the equals of their male counterparts in the work they produced. Even George Eliot conceded that:

> Fiction is a department of literature in which women can, after their kind, fully equal men ... women can produce novels, too, that have a precious speciality, lying quite apart from masculine aptitudes and experience ...
>
> (*Westminster Review*, 1856)

The female imagination, it was observed, was different from the male, more fitted to the portrayal of the variety and pathos of human experience, more geared to influence the moral perceptions of the reading public. George Eliot's own philosophy of writing was shared by many of her sisters. She wrote, she said,

> of mixed human beings in such a way as to call forth tolerant

judgement, pity, and sympathy. And I cannot stir a step aside from what I feel to be true in character.

(Letter to John Blackwood, 1857)

Women novelists, even more than male, directed the moral sympathies of the public, and strengthened the feeling of human solidarity at a time when it was most looked for. Women had, George Eliot remarked, 'genuine observation, humour, and passion' (*Westminster*, 1856), which equipped them to confront what Margaret Oliphant called the 'vexed questions of social morality, and grand problems of human experience' (*Blackwood's*, 1855) which were 'discussed and settled by the novels of the day' – mostly 'written by women'.

In the mid-1850s one group of such women pre-eminently in the minds of both George Eliot and Margaret Oliphant were long-established and well-known names like Currer Bell, Ellis Bell – the pseudonyms of Charlotte and Emily Brontë – and Mrs Gaskell. George Eliot excluded them from her sneers and Margaret Oliphant used them to illustrate her thesis about 'the age of the female novelists'. But in *Blackwood's*, anyway, Oliphant is as enthusiastic about the second rank of women writers, in whose capable hands lay the direction of 'the vexed question' of the day. In their day they were household names. They are not forgotten even today, and some figure prominently among the authors in this book. Charlotte Yonge's *Heir of Redclyffe* was one of the most popular books of the 19th century, and contributed significantly to the religious fervour of the period. Mrs Craik's *John Halifax, Gentleman* became the bible of Victorian upward mobility and secured its author £415 – a considerable sum – in two years. Later in the century, Mrs Humphry Ward's *Robert Elsmere* was reviewed by the Prime Minister and sold 70,000 copies in the first year.

▶ Make a list of the Victorian novels of which you have heard. As far as possible, separate them into the categories defined in Part 1: Approaching the Victorian novel (religious, political, 'industrial novels', etc.). How many were written by women and how many by men? Can you draw any conclusions from your list?

Authorship

It had been an early fear of women novelists that, were critics to know their books were written by women, reviews of their work would be trivialised and serious attention from the public would vanish. This is one reason certainly for the convention of assuming a male pseudonym. Charlotte Brontë in her Biographical Notice to the second edition of *Wuthering Heights*, declared

> ... we veiled our own names under those of Currer, Ellis, and Acton
> Bell ... we had a vague impression that authoresses are liable to be
> looked on with prejudice; we had noticed how critics sometimes use
> for their chastisement the weapon of personality, and for their
> reward, a flattery, which is not true praise.

The Brontë sisters veiled their own names under the ambiguous Currer, Ellis and
Acton Bell through 'a sort of conscientious scruple at assuming names positively
masculine' (Charlotte Brontë). George Eliot had no such scruples, however, and
selected 'George' because it was the name of her partner G.H. Lewes and 'Eliot'
because it was what she called 'a good mouth-filling English name'.

Anonymity, as well as being a form of self-protection, was also a convention by
which the female novelist preserved propriety. Jane Austen had, in an earlier age,
published anonymously; Charlotte Yonge, from a very conservative upper middle-
class family, was only permitted by her parents to publish her first novel,
Abbeychurch (1844), if anonymity was preserved – and if no personal profit
accrued! Elizabeth Gaskell's first novel, *Mary Barton*, was published anonymously.

Conventions of the novel

The conventions under which the Victorian novel flourished can hardly be
dissociated from the reasons for its success, for the one could be seen as leading to
the other – the novelists gave the readers what they wanted. And what the Victorian
public wanted was 'realism'.

'Realism'

It was an age in which 'realism' in art was valued above everything else, though the
meaning of the term shifts as the century goes on. During the 1850s the
daguerreotype (an early kind of photography discovered by Daguerre in Paris in
1839) became fashionable, and in the next twenty years photography developed
into a popular hobby. Photographic reproduction was in the air: the literal
reproduction of life, the importance of 'going back to nature,' became the hallmark
of Victorian taste in art of every kind. On the other hand, of course, nothing must
violate the laws of 'common sense'. Such material was irresistible to the satirist,
and Dickens produced a devastating caricature of the realism of the extreme
literalist in the dialogue between Sissy Jupe and the government officer in *Hard
Times*. When Sissy says she likes carpets with flowers on, she is told this is not
allowed:

> 'You don't walk upon flowers in fact; you cannot be allowed to walk
> upon flowers in carpets,' but only on 'combinations and

modifications ... of mathematical figures which are susceptible of proof and demonstration. This is the new discovery. This is fact. This is taste.'

Realism in art is seen in, for example, Frith's 'Derby Day', a panoramic painting depicting an excited holiday crowd and packed with detail and incident. Realism in the novel is a term used to describe the theory that a novel should reflect in a factual way all the ordinary aspects of human experience, which could be recognised and verified by the reader. (The term had come from France in the 1850s to describe the techniques of Balzac in his *Comedie Humaine* and Flaubert in *Madame Bovary*.) It was the dominating theory of the Victorian period, but was felt most strongly in the middle decades of the century.

Trollope, writing at the end of his professional career, thought of himself as a 'realist':

A novel should give a picture of common life enlivened by humour and sweetened by pathos. To make their [*sic*] picture worthy of attention, the canvas should be crowded with real portraits, not of individuals known to the world or to the author, but of created personages impregnated with traits of character which are known.

(*Autobiography*)

George Eliot wrote a defence of such realism in a famous passage in *Adam Bede* (1859). She talked about the 'precious quality of truthfulness' which she admired in Dutch paintings, the 'faithful pictures of a monotonous homely existence' – village weddings and 'women scraping carrots with their work-worn hands' – on which principle she largely based her own work. She used other conventions too – coincidence, melodrama, the convenient death – which may seem to act against realism, but do not invalidate the principle. (See the extract from *Adam Bede* on pages 79–81.)

Trollope was widely praised throughout his career for his 'truth to nature', his portrayal of character, and his mastery of dialogue – the main features of the realistic school of writing. As one periodical put it, every novelist should have 'the capacity for representing human nature, of creating every figure without life, which to all who see it shall seem to have life, and life of a vivid kind' (*Spectator*, 1865), and Trollope created 'real-life characters' in abundance, whom his readers grew to know and love as their friends. Similarly the stories about the public pressure on Dickens to spare Little Nell in *The Old Curiosity Shop* and Smike in *Nicholas Nickleby* are famous, and illustrate the process of reader-identification with fictional characters.

Dickens, in spite of his enormous popularity, never really belonged to this school of photographic realism, though without question his characters are full of 'life of a vivid kind'. Among his contemporaries, Thackeray observed: 'I don't think [Dickens' art] represents Nature duly.' He felt that Mr Micawber, for example, is 'an exaggeration of a man, as his name is of a name ... I protest against him [Dickens] ... holding the Art of Novels is to represent nature: to convey as strongly as possible the sentiment of reality.' (*Letters*, II) He felt equally strongly about Nancy in *Oliver Twist*: 'the most unreal fantastical personage possible; no more like a thief's mistress' than a Dresden china shepherdess 'resembles a real country wench'.

Thackeray himself, on the other hand, was recognised, like Trollope, as the very embodiment of the realistic school:

> Mr. Thackeray looks at life under its ordinary aspects, and copies it with a fidelity and artistic skill which are surprising. Men, women, and children talk, act, and think in his pages exactly as they are talking acting, and thinking at every hour of the day ...
>
> (*Quarterly Review*, 1865)

The facts and events which form the plot and the background against which the characters are developed were also required to be 'real', and the standard (as for the characters) was again simply external reality. Novelists went to great lengths to establish the accuracy of the details in the plot: as Dickens did over the factual accuracy of the workings of Chancery in *Bleak House*, or George Eliot over the legal ramifications of *Felix Holt* and the 15th-century background of Florence in *Romola*.

▶ How important an ingredient do you think realism should be in a novel? From your own reading would you say that there are important differences between the way Victorian and contemporary writers approach realism in fiction? How large a part does the reader play in accepting the conventions of realism adopted by the author?

The reaction against realism

'Realism' of this rather unsophisticated kind could not satisfy either novelists or critics indefinitely. Dickens was amusing about the convention in *Our Mutual Friend* (1865) when he described Mr Podsnap's taste in literature (and Painting, and Sculpture, and Music) as representations of 'getting up at eight, shaving close at a quarter-past, breakfasting at nine, going to the City at ten, coming home at half-past-five, and dining at seven ...'.

By 1873 the *Westminster* was declaring impatiently:

> Our painting is mere photography, and our descriptive writing is mere topography. Mind is not seen. The play and grace of imagination are lost.

It was also insisting that the true artist must select and shape the materials of his art into a form that reflects his personal vision.

The novelists in the later decades of the century were reacting against the photographic school of realism, and substituting their own versions of 'reality' in more innate, universal terms. Hardy, for instance, though he was punctilious about the accuracy of everyday details in his plot, had a transcendental view of 'realism': he wanted (he said in his *Notebooks*) 'to intensify the expression of things' to bring 'the heart and inner meaning' – fiction was higher than life, and it was not its function to reproduce the minutiae. He pursued the question further in an entry in the *Notebooks* in 1890:

> Art is a disproportioning – (i.e. distorting, throwing out of proportion) – of realities, to show more clearly the features that matter in those realities, which, if merely copied or reported inventorially, might possibly be observed, but would probably be overlooked. Hence 'realism' is not art.

In Hardy – and Meredith, and others – the novel was moving away from exteriority to symbolism and to realism of a different kind.

▶ How easily could Hardy's definition of art and its purpose be applied to Victorian novels you have read?

The author and reader

The question of the author and the narrator he/she employs and their relationship with the reader are other significant areas in the conventions and development of the Victorian novel. The most popular **narrative devices** were those inherited from the 18th century. Two examples are the omniscient author who writes in the third person, and the author who purports to be writing autobiographically, either about the central character of the narrative, or from an 'off-centre' position as another character or as the recipient of the narrative from another source. The Victorian novelist left a permanent mark on each of these narrative devices.

The omniscient narrator

The omniscient narrator, who is the authorial voice, tells the story in the third person. The impersonality and objectivity of the author, which became important conventions in the European and American novel generally, were not widely obvious in the English novel until the influence of France and, in particular, the novelist Gustave Flaubert began to permeate English consciousness later in the century. Flaubert's principle of detaching himself completely from the novel ('A [novelist] must be in his work like God in creation, invisible and all-powerful; he should be everywhere felt, but nowhere seen.' *Selected Letters*) was contested on the English side of the Channel.

For very many Victorians, readers and critics alike, the personality of the narrator was one of the most attractive features of a novel. The narrator, in fact, is a character in his/her own right. This is the case with George Eliot who moves freely, in her own voice, in and out of her narrative, manipulating the response of the reader as she thinks fit. It is the voice of an intelligent, concerned, humorous and thoughtful individual, to whom the reader warms.

Thackeray, too, is his own ringmaster, and talks to his readers with the voice of a relaxed and sophisticated storyteller. He had remarked in *Pendennis* (1848–1850): '[I]n his constant communication with the reader the writer is forced into a frankness of expression, and to speak out his own mind and feelings as they urge him ... It is a sort of confidential talk between writer and reader.' Trollope, another showman, makes a defence of the practice in *Barchester Towers*, where he justifies his intrusion in the novel by saying:

> Our doctrine is, that the author and the reader should move along together in full confidence with each other. Let the personages of the drama undergo ever so complete a comedy of errors among themselves ... but let the spectator ... [never be] one of the dupes.

He invites the reader to share the sense of superiority of the novelist, who is in control, and to collude with the author in the manipulation of the material. (See the extract from *Barchester Towers* on pages 77–78.)

▶ In *Vanity Fair*, Thackeray likened the novelist to a puppeteer, pulling the strings of each character, and then putting the puppets back in their box when the performance was over. What does this suggest to you about the relationship between author, characters and readers?

The first-person narrator

The narrator who writes in the first person was as popular a device in the Victorian novel as it had been the century before, though for different reasons. When Defoe in the 18th century assumed the roles of Robinson Crusoe, Moll Flanders and the Londoner who witnessed the Great Plague of 1665, he did so at least in part to counter the charge that fiction was not 'truth': the narratives were 'fact'. In an age intensely interested in psychology, Dickens wrote as Pip and as David Copperfield, and Charlotte Brontë wrote as Jane Eyre; and one role of the novel was to present the development of a youthful character. This kind of *Bildungsroman* plays a large part in the development of the novel as a form.

It was not the only function of the first-person narrative, however. In *Bleak House* Dickens experimented with the juxtapositioning of Esther's narrative, told in the first person, and the omniscient narrator's account, and he achieved many of his most remarkable effects in this way. With the omniscient narrator, Dickens was able to survey the whole of society and picture the cruelty and selfishness which permeated it at every level. The novel opens famously with the omniscient narrator's description of the fog which – metaphorically – covers England, but is centred most thickly over the High Court of Chancery, the legal heart of England which dominates the story of *Bleak House*. In the parallel narrative, in the voice of the demure, limited and sometimes irritating Esther Summerson, the pace and movement of the novel change regularly as the point of view narrows – the contrast Dickens thus achieves is one of the most striking features of *Bleak House*. He also uses the opportunity to present the dual point of view of crucial incidents in the novel, such as the account of the search for Lady Dedlock.

A different version of first-person narrator is in the voice of another, 'off-centre' character, as in Craik's *John Halifax, Gentleman*, where the narrator is the invalid friend of the hero, Phineas Fletcher. Another example is Samuel Butler's Overton in *The Way of All Flesh*. In both novels the effect is to give an unexpected perspective of the central character. The reader sees John Halifax, the ideal working man and gentle giant, through the eyes of the helpless but better born young Quaker, Phineas; while in Butler's novel the view Overton offers of the central character, Ernest, is that of an older, sophisticated, more worldly friend of the family, who is always a friend and subsequently a role model for Ernest.

Another convention inherited from the early days of the novel was narration through letter, which is a different form of the first person. It had been much used in the 18th century (most notably in the hands of Richardson, where in *Pamela* (1740) and *Clarissa* (1747–1748) the reader, while having access to all the private thoughts of the heroine, could see the shifting points of view without the intrusion of the author) but had ceased to be a popular form a century later. There are a few obvious exceptions, however. The narrative of Anne Brontë's *The Tenant of Wildfell Hall* (1848) is contained in letters, for example; other writers, like Wilkie Collins, in *The Moonstone* and *The Woman in White*, used the technique from time to time.

Different narrative forms: *Wuthering Heights*

One of the most interesting features of *Wuthering Heights* is the series of narrative methods used by Emily Brontë, for the novel is virtually a paradigm of all devices available. All the different narrative forms fit one inside the other, like – as critics have noted – a Chinese box. The principal first-person narrator is Lockwood, the educated, middle-class outsider from the city. His account encloses the whole novel, opening the action with his arrival as Heathcliff's tenant at Thrushcross Grange in 1801, and closing, after a twenty-five year series of flashbacks, shortly after Heathcliff's death in 1802. Inside the outer box of Heathcliff's narrative comes Nelly Dean's narrative: she is another 'off-centre' character – servant, companion, nurse, confidante – who only occasionally has a major part in the action, but who provides Lockwood with the background information of his situation, so that retrospect and present impression continue in counterpoint.

Within these two narratives come other forms, other boxes within boxes. The epistolary convention is represented in Isabella's long letter to Nelly recording her disillusioned dismay with Heathcliff, now her husband ('Is Mr. Heathcliff a man? if so, is he mad? And if not, is he a devil?'). A similar device is Brontë's use of Cathy's diary, which Lockwood reads on his first night at Wuthering Heights.

▶ Look at any two or more Victorian novels with which you are familiar and list the different narrative approaches adopted by the authors. How much are you aware, as a reader, of having your own perspective on the events and characters in the novels manipulated by these different approaches?

The publisher and reader

For much of the 19th century, the working population of Britain was largely illiterate. Until the Education Act of 1870, introduced by W.E. Forster during Gladstone's first term as Prime Minister, education was mainly in the hands of the church. The Church of England, with its 'National Schools', and the Nonconformists, with the 'British and Foreign Schools', educated a small fraction of the nation's children. Even with the local 'dame schools' the majority remained illiterate. However, by the 1890s there had been a succession of reforming acts, education in primary schools had become free and compulsory, and national literacy rose rapidly. A nation of consumers was in preparation for the explosion of the book trade which marked the second half of the century.

'Three-decker' novels

For much of this time, however, the novels that might have gratified the taste of the new readers remained prohibitively expensive. The convention, at the start of the Victorian period, was to publish new novels in three volumes, at 10/6d (just over 50 pence) per volume, or 'a guinea and a half' per novel. Charlotte Brontë found that her first novel – in one volume – had little success with publishers, but a kindly letter from another firm, Smith and Elder, informed her that 'a work in three volumes would meet with careful attention' (Biographical Note to the Second Edition of *Wuthering Heights*). The price of a novel to a working man or woman was often more than a week's wages, and the 'three-decker' remained firmly out of reach of much of the population, and not simply the working class.

Mudie's lending library

For the middle classes Mudie's lending library was the answer. Charles Edward Mudie was one of the great Victorian entrepreneurs of fiction: in 1842, when he was scarcely twenty-four, he hit on the idea of making all the resources of the Victorian book trade, particularly the novel, available to the reading public for the price of one guinea (£1.10) a year, dramatically undercutting all rivals. For less than two-thirds the price of one novel, the reader could enjoy as many as came out in the year. Moreover, Mudie was reliable: what he offered was a 'Select Library'. Nothing which could embarrass a parent or distress a young person was accepted. And he rapidly gained such prestige and such power that the success or failure of a novel came to depend on Mudie's approbation. As guaranteed family reading Mudie's books became a regular factor in publishers' calculations – a novel which failed the Mudie test and was rejected from the lending libraries, faced a very uncertain future.

The 'railway boom' between 1844 and 1847 gave a great boost to the fortunes of the lending library and a captive market to Mudie. With 3000 miles added to existing track by 1845, a long train journey was likely to occupy a reader the length of one volume!

W.H. Smith, another young entrepreneur, was also in the race. He secured the monopoly of railway bookstalls on the London and North-Western Systems and opened the first on the new Euston Station in 1848.

The publishers, too, cashed in on the boom by issuing quantities of cheap reprints. Routledge, for instance, issued the 'Railway Library' editions in 1848, and Bentley's 'Shilling Series' and 'Railway Library' came out in 1852–1853.

Serial publication

Serial publication, and publication in monthly numbers, were other means by which publishers attracted the custom of readers. A long novel could be bought in instalments and, again, for far less than the price of a conventional 'three-decker'. The novelist, too, benefited from this system, and shared in the profits. A successful novelist like Dickens could become wealthy on serial publication, and this fact alone raised the status of the profession and the novelist.

In accordance with this trend, the middle decades of the century saw a dramatic rise in the appearance of periodicals which serialised new fiction. After the runaway success of *The Pickwick Papers* in monthly numbers by Smith and Elder in 1836, most of the major publishers produced their own 'house' periodical (for example, Blackwood, Macmillan and Tinsley). Most of the major novelists published work in this form. Dickens published nearly all his novels like this, Thackeray a majority, and Trollope, Gaskell, George Eliot, Wilkie Collins and Meredith a number.

Novelists were editors, too, and published their own work: Dickens edited *All the Year Round* and *Household Words*; Trollope, *St. Paul's Magazine*. Thackeray was the first editor of the *Cornhill*; M.E. Braddon edited *Belgravia* and Mrs Humphry Ward, *Argosy*, while Charlotte Yonge was the editor of the *Monthly Packet* for more than forty years.

Publishers who took serials could also, like the editors of the journals, dictate the shape of the fiction they brought out. Dickens' quarrels with Elizabeth Gaskell over the length and episodes of her novels and stories were famous.

Parodies

One significant mode of discourse by which it is possible to understand how a work was received (usually by later generations of readers) is found in the parodies of a text or an author that appear subsequently. They can be savage or affectionate, but always foreground (give particular emphasis to) the features which appear most obvious in retrospect, thus indicating a later reception of the text, and its familiarity with the reading public.

The Victorian era was the golden age of parody: it flourished as an art form in its own right, and, it was said, '[n]o age and no country can show anything approaching the combined sparkle and finish of the mid-Victorian parodists' (D. Macdonald *Parodies*). The Victorians famously parodied contemporary poets (highlighting, for example, the outstanding characteristics of Wordsworth, Browning and Tennyson), but the novelists were caught most successfully by a late-Victorian parodist, Max Beerbohm. His finest collection of parodies, *A Christmas Garland*, was published in 1912, though many of the individual pieces on different novelists had been written much earlier. And when the Victorian novel became grist to the mill of the various modern, late 20th-century schools of criticism, the parodies of the different critics offer another illuminating view of the novels themselves. (See Beerbohm's 'The Feast' on pages 86–88; also Part 4: Critical approaches.)

Some authors and texts are more obvious targets for parody than others: Dickens and Hardy are notable victims, though Conrad and Meredith do not escape. Robert Benchley, a well-known American parodist, writing in the *New Yorker* in the 1950s, picks up the arch tone of Dickens' relentless bonhomie in *A Christmas Carol* in his description of Christmas afternoon with the Gummidge family:

> What an afternoon! Mr Gummidge said that, in his estimation, there never had been such an afternoon since the world began, a sentiment which was heavily endorsed by Mrs Gummidge and all the little

Gummidges, not to mention the relatives who had come over from Jersey for the day.

In the first place, there was the ennui. And such ennui as it was! A heavy, overpowering ennui, such as results from ... eight courses of steaming, gravied food ... a dragging, revitalising ennui ... an ennui which carried with it a retinue of yawns, snarls, and thinly-veiled insults, and which ended in ruptures in the clan spirit serious enough to last throughout the glad new year ... Then there was the cigar smoke! Mrs Gummidge said she didn't mind the smoke from a good cigarette, but would they mind if she opened the window for just a minute in order to clear the room of the heavy aroma of used cigars? ...

And as Tiny Tim might say in speaking of Christmas afternoon as an institution, 'God help us, every one'

(quoted in D. Macdonald *Parodies,* 1954)

An unexpected parodist of Dickens' sententious sentimentality is James Joyce. In a section of *Ulysses* made up of parodies of earlier literature, the birth of Mrs Purefoy's baby is brought to the reader as though from Dickens:

Meanwhile the skill and patience of the physician had brought about a happy accouchement ... She had fought the good fight and now she was very very happy. Those who have passed on, who have gone before, are happy too as they gaze down upon the touching scene. Reverently look at her as she reclines there with the motherlight in her eyes, that longing hunger for baby fingers (a pretty sight to see), in the first flush of her new motherhood, breathing a silent prayer of the One above, the Universal Husband ...

('The Oxen in the Sun', *Ulysses*)

Dickens and Hardy were, in the words of a much earlier parodist, James Smith, 'writers whose style and habit of thought, being more marked and peculiar, were more capable of exaggeration and distortion' (*Rejected Addresses*, 1812). In their pursuit of the 'marked and peculiar', parodists were sometimes able to highlight essential features of the original. Stella Gibbons produced a devastating parody of one side of Hardy and his imitators in *Cold Comfort Farm* in 1932. In her pictures of how a sophisticated young urban dweller confronts and engages with life in a rugged rural setting inhabited by elemental figures, she is using a technique made familiar by Emily Brontë in *Wuthering Heights* – Flora Poste and Lockwood have a common background. Wuthering Heights and Cold Comfort Farm also share a possible source: Cold Comfort Farm 'crouched like a beast about to spring, under the bulk of Mock-uncle hill'. Wuthering Heights is flanked by 'gaunt thorns all stretching their limbs one way, as if craving alms of the sun'. When it comes to the characters, Seth Starkadder, whose voice had 'a low throaty, animal quality, a sneering warmth that wound a ribbon of sexuality over the outward coarseness of the man ...', is of the earth.

The setting of the farm is heavy with doom:

> All the surrounding surface of the countryside – the huddled Downs lost in rain, the wet fields fanged abruptly with flints, the leafless thorns thrust sideways by the eternal pawing of the wind, the lush brooding miles of meadow through which the lifeless river wandered – seemed to be folding inwards upon themselves. Their dumbness said 'Give up. There is no answer to the riddle ...

The setting is also strongly reminiscent of Flintcomb-Ash (in *Tess of the d'Urbervilles*) or of Egdon Heath (in *The Return of the Native*), as described here:

> The heath wore the appearance of an instalment of night which had taken up its place before its astronomical hour had come ... The face of the heath, by its mere complexion added half an hour to evening; it could in like manner retard the dawn, sadden noon, anticipate the frowning of storms scarcely generated, and intensify the opacity of a moonless midnight to a cause of shaking and dread ... the storm was its lover, and the wind its friend. Then it became the home of strange phantoms; and it was found to be the hitherto unrecognised original of those wild regions of obscurity which are vaguely felt to be encompassing about in midnight dreams of flight and disaster ...

In the characters of Adam Lambsbreath and some of the remoter Starkadder relations like Urk and Micah, Stella Gibbons plays with Hardy's idea of timeless figures who spring from the environment and remain part of it. Hardy's grotesque figure of Diggory Venn, the reddleman, here conducts his 'lurid' cart across the heath:

> ... like his van he was completely red ... The traveller with the cart was a reddleman ... one of a class rapidly becoming extinct in Wessex, filling at present in the rural world the place which, during the last century, the dodo occupied in the world of animals. He is a curious, interesting, and nearly perished link between obsolete forms of life and those which finally prevail.
>
> (*Return of the Native*)

Assignments

1 Choose a novel you know well and try to write a parody of the style in which it is written. What do you learn about the techniques used by the original writer from your parodying of his or her style?

2 Choose two novels by different writers and select from one of the novels an episode or character. Now try to rewrite the episode or present the character in the style of the second writer. If working with others, you could produce re-writings of a variety of novels and see how easily each one can be identified.

3 Select a novel which was originally published either in serial or 'three-decker' format. Look carefully at the endings of each part or volume (these breaks are often indicated in modern editions of the books). Do the breaks come at apparently arbitrary points or are they placed at strategic moments in the development of the plot? Compare the ways in which television adaptations of Victorian novels divide the story up into episodes or parts. How closely have the television screenwriters been able to follow the serial divisions of the original?

4 Focusing on one novel you have read, write a review as if you were reviewing the novel on its first appearance, for example, *Vanity Fair* in 1848 or *The Mayor of Casterbridge* in 1886.

5 A number of Victorian novels are set in a period well before their actual date of composition: *Wuthering Heights*, for instance, is set in 1801 and deals with events of an even earlier date. Do you think these novels nevertheless offer an insight into the attitudes and values of the Victorian era? What, do you think, were the motives of the novelists in choosing to present their material in this way?

3 | Texts and extracts

The texts and extracts that follow have been chosen to illustrate key themes and points made elsewhere in the book, and to provide material which may be useful when working on the assignments. The items are arranged chronologically.

Thomas Carlyle

From 'Signs of the Times' (1829)

In an early essay which anticipates important areas of Victorian thinking, Carlyle warns his readers of the way he sees society developing.

> Were we required to characterise this age of ours by any single epithet, we should we tempted to call it, not an Heroical, Devotional, Philosophical, or Moral Age, but, above all others, the Mechanical Age. It is the Age of Machinery, in every outward and inward sense of that word; the age which, with its whole undivided might, forwards, teaches and practises the great art of adapting means to ends. Nothing is now done directly, or by hand; all is by rule and calculated contrivance. ...
>
> ... Not the external and physical alone is now managed by machinery, but the internal and spiritual also. Here too nothing follows its spontaneous course, nothing is left to be accomplished by old natural methods. Everything has its cunningly devised implements, its pre-established apparatus, it is not done by hand but by machinery. ... It is the same in all departments. Has any man, or any society of men, a truth to speak, a piece of spiritual work to do; they can nowise proceed at once and with the mere natural organs, but must first call a public meeting, appoint committees, issue prospectuses, eat a public dinner; in a word, construct or borrow machinery, wherewith to speak it and do it. ...
>
> In fact, if we look deeper, we shall find that this faith in Mechanism has now struck its roots down into man's most intimate, primary sources of conviction; and is thence sending up, over his whole life and activity, innumerable stems, - fruit-bearing and poison-bearing. The truth is, men have lost their belief in the Invisible, and believe, and hope, and work only in the Visible; or, to speak it in other words: This is not a Religious age. Only the material, the immediately practical, not the divine and spiritual, is important to us. The infinite, absolute character of Virtue has passed into a finite, conditional one; it is no longer a worship of the Beautiful and Good; but a calculation of the Profitable. Worship, indeed, in any sense, is not recognised

among us, or is mechanically explained into Fear of pain, or Hope of pleasure. Our true Deity is Mechanism. It has subdued external Nature for us, and we think it will do all other things. We are Giants in physical power: in a deeper than metaphorical sense, we are Titans, that strive, by heaping mountain on mountain, to conquer Heaven also.

From *Past and Present* (1843)

Carlyle juxtaposes the Hero of the Past (Abbot Samson of St Edmundsbury) with the Hero of the Present (the Captain of Industry, Plugson of Undershot), and the sets of values which each represents. Here Carlyle is inviting the reader to condemn, as he does, the materialistic ethic represented by Plugson which, he feels, characterises contemporary society.

> Cash-payment never was, or could except for a few years be, the union-bond of man to man. Cash never yet paid one man fully his deserts to another; nor could it, nor can it, now or henceforth to the end of the world. I invite his Grace of Castle-Rackrent to reflect on this; - does he think that a Land Aristocracy when it becomes a Land Auctioneership can have long to live? Or that Sliding-scales will increase the vital stamina of it? The indomitable Plugson too, of the respected Firm of Plugson, Hunks and Company in St. Dolly Undershot, is invited to reflect on this; for to him also it will be new, perhaps even newer. Book-keeping by double entry is admirable, and records several things in an exact manner. But the Mother-Destinies also keep their Tablets; in Heaven's Chancery also there goes on a recording; and things, as my Moslem friends say, are 'written on the iron leaf'.
>
> Your Grace and Plugson, it is like, go to Church occasionally: did you never in vacant moments, with perhaps a dull parson droning to you, glance into your New Testament, and the cash-account stated four times over, by a kind of quadruple entry, - in the Four Gospels there? I consider that a cash-account, and balance-statement of work done and wages paid, worth attending to. Precisely *such*, though on a smaller scale, go on at all moments under this Sun; and the statement and balance of them in the Plugson Ledgers and on the Tablets of Heaven's Chancery are discrepant exceedingly; - which ought really to teach, and to have long since taught, an indomitable common-sense Plugson of Undershot, much more an unattackable *un*common-sense Grace of Rackrent, a thing or two! - In brief, we shall have to dismiss the Cash-Gospel rigorously into its own place: we shall have to know, on the threshold, that either there is some

infinitely deeper Gospel, subsidiary, explanatory and daily and hourly corrective, to the Cash one; or else that the Cash one itself and all others are fast travelling! ...

A human being who has worked with human beings clears all scores with them, cuts himself with triumphant completeness for ever loose from them, by paying down certain shillings and pounds. Was it not the wages I promised you? There they are, to the last sixpence, - according to the Laws of the Bucaniers! - Yes, indeed; - and, at such times, it becomes imperatively necessary to ask all persons, bucaniers and others, Whether these same respectable Laws of the Bucaniers are written on God's eternal Heavens at all, on the inner Heart of Man at all; or on the respectable Bucanier Logbook merely, for the convenience of bucaniering merely? What a question; - whereat Westminster Hall shudders to its driest parchment; and on the dead wigs each particular horsehair stands on end!

Charlotte Brontë

From *Jane Eyre* (1847)

Charlotte Brontë explores the question of self-identity throughout *Jane Eyre*, and it is a regular theme in the Victorian novel. This is a dramatic moment in her treatment of the topic.

'One instant, Jane. Give one glance to my horrible life when you are gone. All happiness will be torn away with you. What then is left? For a wife I have but the maniac upstairs: as well might you refer me to some corpse in yonder churchyard. What shall I do, Jane? Where turn for a companion, and for some hope?'

'Do as I do: trust in God and yourself. Believe in heaven. Hope to meet again there.'

'Then you will not yield?'

'No.'

'Then you condemn me to live wretched, and to die accursed?' His voice rose.

'I advise you to live sinless; and I wish you to die tranquil.'

'Then you snatch love and innocence from me? You fling me back on lust for a passion – vice for an occupation?'

'Mr. Rochester, I no more assign this fate to you than I grasp at it for myself. We were born to strive and endure – you as well as I: do so. You will forget me before I forget you.'

'You make me a liar by such language: you sully my honour. I declared I could not change: you tell me to my face I shall change soon. And what a distortion in your judgment, what a perversity in your ideas, is proved by your conduct! Is it better to drive a fellow-creature to despair than to transgress a mere human law – no man being injured by the breach? for you to have neither relatives nor acquaintances whom you need fear to offend by living with me.'

This was true and while he spoke my very conscience and reason turned traitors against me, and charged me with crime in resisting him. They spoke almost as loud as Feeling: and that clamoured wildly. 'Oh, comply!' it said. 'Think of his misery; think of his danger – look at his state when left alone; remember his headlong nature; consider the recklessness following on despair – soothe him; save him; love him; tell him you love him and will be his. Who in the world cares for *you*? or who will be injured by what you do?'

Still indomitable was the reply – '*I* care for myself. The more solitary, the more friendless, the more unsustained I am, the more I will respect myself. I will keep the laws given by God; sanctioned by man. I will hold to the principles received by me when I was sane, and not mad – as I am now. Laws and principles are not for the times when there is no temptation: they are for such moments as this, when body and soul rise in mutiny against their rigour; stringent are they; inviolate they shall be. If at my individual convenience I might break them, what would be their worth? They have a worth – so I have always believed; and if I cannot believe it now, it is because I am insane – quite insane: with my veins running fire, and my heart beating faster than I can count its throbs. Preconceived opinions, foregone determinations, are all I have at this hour to stand by: there I plant my foot.'

I did.

John Henry Newman

From *Loss and Gain* (1848)

This extract – and the one from Mrs Humphry Ward's *Robert Elsmere* on pages 84–85 – illustrates the extremes of religious controversy as represented in the novel: in this, it is the ecstasy of conversion.

It was Sunday morning about seven o'clock, and Charles had been admitted into the communion of the Catholic Church about an hour since. He was still kneeling in the church of the Passionists before the Tabernacle, in the possession of a deep peace and serenity of mind, which he had not thought possible on earth. It was more like the stillness which almost sensibly affects the ears when a bell that has long been tolling stops, or when a vessel, after much tossing at sea, finds itself in harbour. It was such as to throw him back in memory on his earliest years, as if he were really beginning life again. But there was more than the happiness of childhood in his heart; he seemed to feel a rock under his feet; it was the *soliditas Cathedra Petri*. He went on kneeling, as if he were already in heaven, with the throne of God before him, and angels around, and as if to move were to lose his privilege.

At length he felt a light hand on his shoulder, and a voice said, 'Reding, I am going; let me just say farewell to you before I go.' He looked around; it was Willis, or rather Father Aloysius, in his dark Passionist habit, with the white heart sewed in at his left breast. Willis carried him from the church into the sacristy. 'What a joy, Reding!' he whispered, when the door closed upon them; 'what a day of joy! St Edward's day, a doubly blessed day henceforth. My superior let me be present; but now I must go. You did not see me, but I was present through the whole.'

'O,' said Charles, 'what shall I say? – the face of God! As I knelt I seemed to wish to say this, and this only, with the Patriarch, "Now let me die, since I have seen Thy Face".'

'You, dear Reding,' said Father Aloysius, 'have keen fresh feelings; mine are blunted by familiarity.'

'No, Willis,' he made answer,' you have taken the better part betimes, while I have loitered. Too late have I known Thee, O Thou ancient Truth; too late have I found Thee, First and only Fair.'

'All is well, except as sin makes it ill,' said Father Aloysius; 'if you have to lament loss of time before conversion, I have to lament it after. If you speak of delay, must not I of rashness? A good God overrules all things. But I must away. Do you recollect my last words when we parted in Devonshire? I have thought of them often since; they were too true then. I said, "Our ways divide." They are different still, yet they are the same. Whether we shall meet again here below, who knows? but there will be a meeting ere long before the Throne of God, and under the shadow of His Blessed Mother and all Saints. "Deus manifeste veniet, Deus noster, et non silebit."'

Reding took Father Aloysius's hand and kissed it; as he sank on his knees the young priest made the sign of the blessing over him. Then he vanished through the door of the sacristy; and the new convert sought his temporary cell, so happy in the Present, that he had no thoughts either for the Past or the Future.

Charles Dickens

From *David Copperfield* (1849–1850)

In this passage Dickens gently mocks, through the character of David at this stage in his development, the conventions of bourgeois Utilitarianism, where all judgements are made in commercial terms. They are conventions very obvious in many early Victorian novels.

I have come legally to man's estate. I have attained the dignity of twenty-one. But this is a sort of dignity that may be thrust upon one. Let me think what I have achieved.

I have tamed that savage stenographic mystery. I make a respectable income by it. I am in high repute for my accomplishment in all pertaining to the art, and am joined with eleven others in reporting the debates in Parliament for a Morning Newspaper. Night after night, I record predictions that never come to pass, professions that are never fulfilled, explanations that are only meant to mystify. I wallow in words. Britannia, that unfortunate female, is always before me, like a trussed fowl: skewered through and through with office-pens, and bound hand and foot with red tape. I am sufficiently behind the scenes to know the worth of political life. I am quite an Infidel about it, and shall never be converted.

My dear old Traddles has tried his hand at the same pursuit, but it is not in Traddle's way. He is perfectly good-humoured respecting his failure, and reminds me that he always did consider himself slow. He has occasional employment on the same newspaper, in getting up the facts of dry subjects, to be written about and embellished by more fertile minds. He is called to the bar; and with admirable industry and self-denial has scraped another hundred pounds together, to fee a Conveyancer whose chambers he attends. A great deal of very hot port wine was consumed at his call; and, considering the figure, I should think the Inner Temple must have made a profit by it.

I have come out in another way. I have taken with fear and trembling to authorship. I wrote a little something, in secret, and sent it to a magazine, and it was published in the magazine. Since then, I have taken heart to write a good many trifling pieces. Now, I am regularly paid for them. Altogether, I am well off; when I tell my income on the fingers of my left hand, I pass the third finger and take in the fourth to the middle joint.

We have removed, from Buckingham Street, to a pleasant little cottage very near the one I looked at, when my enthusiasm first came on. My aunt, however (who has sold the house at Dover, to good advantage), is not going to remain here, but intends removing herself to a still more tiny cottage close at hand. What does this portend? My marriage yes? Yes!

Yes! I am going to be married to Dora. Miss Lavinia and Miss Clarissa have given their consent; and if ever canary birds were in a flutter, they are.

From *Hard Times* (1854)

In both these passages Dickens is offering a satirical view of how the Utilitarian rejection of everything outside the immediately practical or useful is blighting society at its roots: there is something else in life, he insists (and Sissy knows what it is), that they will ignore at their peril.

The third gentleman now stepped forth. ...

"This is a new principle, a discovery, a great discovery," said the gentleman. ... Suppose you were going to carpet a room. Would you use a carpet having a representation of flowers upon it?"

There being a general conviction by this time that "No, Sir!" was always the right answer to this gentleman, the chorus of No was very strong. Only a few feeble stragglers said Yes: among them Sissy Jupe.

"Girl number twenty," said the gentleman, smiling in his calm strength of knowledge.

Sissy blushed, and stood up.

"So you would carpet your room – or your husband's room, if you were a grown woman, and had a husband – with representations of flowers, would you?" said the gentleman. "Why would you?"

"If you please, Sir, I am very fond of flowers," returned the girl.

"And is that why you would put tables and chairs upon them, and have people walking over them with heavy boots?"

"It wouldn't hurt them, Sir. They wouldn't crush and wither, if you please, Sir. They would be the pictures of what was very pretty and pleasant, and I would fancy -"

"Ay, ay, ay! But you mustn't fancy," cried the gentleman, quite elated by coming so happily to his point. "That's it! You are never to fancy."

"You are not, Cecilia Jupe," Thomas Gradgrind solemnly repeated, "to do anything of that kind."

"Fact, fact, fact!" said the gentleman. And "Fact, fact, fact!" repeated Thomas Gradgrind.

"You are to be in all things regulated and governed," said the gentleman, "by fact. We hope to have, before long, a board of fact, composed of commissioners of fact, who will force the people to be a people of fact, and of nothing but fact. You must discard the word Fancy altogether. You have nothing to do with it. You are not to have, in any object of use or ornament, what would be a contradiction in fact. You don't walk upon flowers in fact; you cannot be allowed to walk upon flowers in carpets. You don't find that foreign birds and butterflies come and perch upon your crockery; you cannot be permitted to paint foreign birds and butterflies upon your crockery. You never meet with quadrupeds going up and down walls; you must not have quadrupeds represented upon walls. You must use," said the gentleman, "for all these purposes, combinations and modifications (in primary colours) of mathematical figures which are susceptible of proof and demonstration. This is the new discovery. This is fact. This is taste." …

*   *   *   *   *   *   *   *

Left alone with her mother, Louisa saw her lying with an awful lull upon her face, like one who was floating away upon some great water, all resistance over, content to be carried down the stream. She put the shadow of a hand to her lips again, and recalled her.

"You were going to speak to me, mother." …

"You must remember, my dear, that whenever I have said anything, on any subject, I have never heard the last of it: and consequently, that I have long left off saying anything."

"I can hear you, mother." But, it was only by dint of bending down to her ear, and at the same time attentively watching the lips as they moved, that she could link such faint and broken sounds into any chain of connexion.

"You learnt a great deal, Louisa, and so did your brother. Ologies of all kinds from morning to night. If there is any Ology left, of any description, that has not been worn to rags in this house, all I can say is, I hope I shall never hear its name."

"I can hear you, mother, when you have strength to go on." This, to keep her from floating away.

"But, there is something – not an Ology at all – that your father has missed, or forgotten, Louisa. I don't know what it is. I have often sat with Sissy near me, and thought about it. I shall never get its name now. But your father may. It makes me restless. I want to write to him, to find out for God's sake, what it is. Give me a pen, give me a pen."

Even the power of restlessness was gone, except from the poor head, which could just turn from side to side.

She fancied, however, that her request had been complied with, and that the pen she could not have held was in her hand. It matters little what figures of wonderful no-meaning she began to trace upon her wrappers. The hand soon stopped in the midst of them; the light that had always been feeble and dim behind the weak transparency, went out; and even Mrs. Gradgrind, emerged from the shadow in which man walketh and disquieteth himself in vain, took upon her the dread solemnity of the sages and patriarchs.

Anthony Trollope

From *Barchester Towers* (1857)

Here Trollope has adopted as the authorial voice the relaxed tones of a friend explaining his view of the author/reader relationship. The author is taking part in his own novel, and addresses the reader as one intelligent humane person to another.

> ... let the gentle-hearted reader be under no apprehension whatsoever. It is not destined that Eleanor shall marry Mr. Slope or Bertie Stanhope. And here, perhaps, it may be allowed to the novelist to explain his views on a very important point in the art of telling tales. He ventures to reprobate that system which goes so far to violate all proper confidence between the author and his readers, by maintaining nearly to the end of the third volume a mystery as to the fate of their favourite personage. Nay, more, and worse than this, is too frequently done. Have not often the profoundest efforts of genius been used to baffle the aspirations of the reader, to raise false hopes and false fears, and to give rise to expectations which are never to be realised? Are not promises all but made of delightful horrors, in lieu of which the writer produces nothing but most commonplace realities in his final chapter? And is there not a species of deceit in this to which the honesty of the present age should lend no countenance?
>
> And what can be the worth of that solicitude which a peep into the third volume can utterly dissipate? What the value of those literary charms which are absolutely destroyed by their enjoyment? When we have once learnt what was that picture before which was hung Mrs. Ratcliffe's solemn curtain, we feel no further interest about either the frame or the veil. They are to us, merely a receptacle for old bones, an inappropriate coffin, which we would wish to have decently buried out of our sight.
>
> And then, how grievous a thing it is to have the pleasure of your novel destroyed by the ill-considered triumph of a previous reader.

'Oh. You needn't be alarmed for Augusta, of course she accepts Gustavus in the end.' 'How very ill-natured you are, Susan,' says Kitty, with tears in her eyes; 'I don't care a bit about it now.' Dear Kitty, if you will read my book, you may defy the ill-nature of your sister. There shall be no secret that she can tell you. Nay, take the last chapter if you please – learn from its pages all the results of our troubled story, and the story shall have lost none of its interest, if indeed there be any interest in it to lose.

Our doctrine is, that the author and the reader should move along together in full confidence with each other. Let the personages of the drama undergo ever so complete a comedy of errors among themselves, but let the spectator never mistake the Syracusan for the Ephesian; otherwise he is one of the dupes, and the part of a dupe is never dignified.

I would not for the value of this chapter have it believed by a single reader that my Eleanor could bring herself to marry Mr. Slope, or that she should be sacrificed to a Bertie Stanhope. But among the good folk of Barchester many believed both the one and the other.

Dinah Mulock (Mrs Craik)

From *John Halifax, Gentleman* (1857)

The class-barriers that divided Victorian society, and individual attempts to cross them, are a favourite theme in Victorian fiction. Dinah Mulock's *John Halifax, Gentleman* is a well-known example.

"This is not a very long good-bye, I trust?" said she to me, with something more than courtesy. "I shall remain at the Mythe House some weeks, I believe. How long do you purpose staying at Enderley?"

I was uncertain.

"But your home is in Norton Bury? I hope – I trust, you will allow my cousin to express in his own house his thanks and mine for your great kindness during my trouble?"

Neither of us answered. Miss March looked surprised – hurt – nay, displeased; then her eye, resting on John, lost its haughtiness, and became humble and sweet.

"Mr. Halifax, I know nothing of my cousin, and I do know you. Will you tell me – candidly, as I know you will – whether there is anything in Mr. Brithwood which you think unworthy of your acquaintance?"

"He would think me unworthy of his," was the low, firm answer.

Miss March smiled incredulously. "Because you are not very rich?

What can that signify? It is enough for me that my friends are gentlemen."

"Mr. Brithwood, and many others, would not allow my claim to that title."

Astonished – nay, somewhat more than astonished – the young gentlewoman drew back a little. "I do not quite understand you."

"Let me explain, then," and her involuntary gesture seeming to have brought back all honest dignity and manly pride, he faced her, once more himself. "It is right, Miss March, that you should know who and what I am, to whom you are giving the honour of your kindness. Perhaps you ought to have known before; but here at Enderley we seemed to be equals – friends."

"I have indeed felt it so."

"Then you will the sooner pardon my not telling you – what you never asked, and I was only too ready to forget – that we are *not* equals – that is, society would not regard us as such – and I doubt if even you yourself would wish us to be friends."

"Why not?"

"Because you are a gentlewoman and I am a tradesman."

The news was evidently a shock to her – it could not but be, reared as she had been. She sat – the eyelashes dropping over her flushed cheeks – perfectly silent.

John's voice grew firmer – prouder – no hesitation, now.

"My calling is, as you will soon hear at Norton Bury, that of a tanner. I am apprentice to Abel Fletcher – Phineas's father."

"Mr Fletcher!" She looked up at me – a mingled look of kindliness and pain.

"Ay, Phineas is a little less beneath your notice than I am. He is rich – he has been well educated; I have had to educate myself. I came to Norton Bury six years ago – a beggar boy. No, not quite that – for I never begged! I either worked or starved."

The earnestness, the passion of his tone, made Miss March lift her eyes …

George Eliot

From *Adam Bede* (1859)

George Eliot is here putting the case for the sort of realism, the 'quality of truthfulness', that she believes the novelist should aim for.

Falsehood is so easy, truth so difficult. The pencil is conscious of a delightful facility in drawing a griffin – the longer the claws, and the larger the wings, the better; but that marvellous facility which we mistook for genius is apt to forsake us when we want to draw a real, unexaggerated lion. Examine your words well, and you will find that even when you have no motive to be false, it is a very hard thing to say the exact truth, even about your own immediate feelings – much harder than to say something fine about them which is *not* the exact truth.

It is for this rare, precious quality of truthfulness that I delight in many Dutch paintings, which lofty-minded people despise. I find a source of delicious sympathy in these faithful pictures of a monotonous homely existence, which has been the fate of so many more among my fellow-mortals than a life of pomp or of absolute indigence, of tragic suffering, or of world-stirring actions. I turn without shrinking from cloudborne angels, from prophets, sibyls, and heroic warriors, to an old woman bending over her flowerpot, or eating her solitary dinner, while the noonday light, softened perhaps by a screen of leaves, falls on her mob-cap, and just touches the rim of her spinning-wheel, and her stone jug, and all those cheap, common things which are the precious necessities of life to her; or I turn to that village wedding, kept between four brown walls; where an awkward bridegroom opens the dance with a high-shouldered, broad-faced bride, while elderly and middle-aged friends look on, with very irregular noses and lips, and probably with quart-pots in their hands, but with an expression of unmistakable contentment and good-will. 'Foh!' says my idealistic friend, 'what vulgar details! What good is there in taking all these pains to give an exact likeness of old women and clowns? What a low phase of life! - what clumsy, ugly people!'

But, bless us, things may be lovable that are not altogether handsome, I hope? I am not at all sure that the majority of the human race have not been ugly, and even among those 'lords of their kind,' the British, squat figures, ill-shapen nostrils, and dingy complexions are not startling exceptions. Yet there is a great deal of family love amongst us. I have a friend or two whose class of features is such that the Apollo curl on the summit of their brows would be decidedly trying; yet to my certain knowledge tender hearts have beaten for them, and their miniatures – flattering, but still not lovely – are kissed in secret by motherly lips. I have seen many an excellent matron, who could never in her best days have been handsome, and yet she had a packet of yellow love-letters in a private drawer, and sweet children showered kisses on her sallow cheeks. And I believe there have been plenty of young heroes, of middle stature and feeble beards, who have felt quite sure they could never love anything more insignificant than a Diana, and yet have found themselves in middle life happily settled with a wife who waddles. Yes! thank God; human feeling is like the mighty rivers that bless the earth: it does not wait for beauty – it flows with resistless force and brings beauty with it.

From *Felix Holt*, the 'Address to Working Men' (1866)

George Eliot added Felix Holt's 'Address to Working Men' to the novel at the request of the publishers. Here she makes explicit the message of the novel, and her conviction that all change must be gradual and the result of careful preparation and education.

I am a Radical; and what is more, I am not a Radical with a title, or a French cook, or even an entrance into fine society. I expect great changes, and I desire them. But I don't expect them to come in a hurry, by mere inconsiderate sweeping. A Hercules with a big besom is a fine thing for a filthy stable, but not for weeding a seed-bed, where his besom would soon make a barren floor.

That is old-fashioned talk, some one may say. We know all that.

Yes, when things are put in an extreme way, most people think they know them; but, after all, they are comparatively few who see the small degrees by which those extremes are arrived at, or have the resolution and self-control to resist the little impulses by which they creep on surely towards a fatal end. Does anybody set out meaning to ruin himself, or to drink himself to death, or to waste his life so that he becomes a despicable old man, a super-annuated nuisance, like a fly in winter? Yet there are plenty, of whose lot this is the pitiable story. Well now, supposing us all to have the best intentions, we working men, as a body, run some risk of bringing evil on the nation in that unconscious manner – half-hurrying, half-pushed in a jostling march towards an end we are not thinking of. For just as there are many things which we know better and feel much more strongly than the richer, softer-handed classes can know or feel them; so there are many things – many precious benefits – which we, by the very fact of our privations, our lack of leisure and instruction, are not so likely to be aware of and take into our account. Those precious benefits form a chief part of what I may call the common estate of society: a wealth over and above buildings, machinery, produce, shipping, and so on, though closely connected with these; a wealth of a more delicate kind, that we may more unconsciously bring into danger, doing harm and not knowing that we do it. I mean that treasure of knowledge, science, poetry, refinement of thought, feeling, and manners, great memories and the interpretation of great records, which is carried on from the minds of one generation to the minds of another. This is something distinct from the indulgences of luxury and the pursuit of vain finery; and one of the hardships in the lot of working men is that they have been for the most part shut out from sharing in this treasure. It can make a man's life very great, very full of delight, though he has no smart furniture and no horses: it also yields a great deal of discovery that corrects error, and of invention that lessens bodily pain, and must at last make life easier for all.

... You may truly say that this which I call the common estate of society has been anything but common to you; but the same may be said, by many of us, of the sunlight and the air, of the sky and the fields, of parks and holiday games. Nevertheless, that these blessings exist makes life worthier to us, and urges us the more to energetic, likely means of getting our share in them; and I say, let us watch carefully, lest we do anything to lessen this treasure which is held in the minds of men, while we exert ourselves first of all, and to the very utmost, that we and our children may share in all its benefits. Yes; exert ourselves to the utmost, to break the yoke of ignorance. ... Without this no political measures can benefit us. No political institution will alter the nature of Ignorance, or hinder it from producing vice and misery. Let Ignorance start how it will, it must run the same round of low appetites, poverty, slavery and superstition.

Anthony Trollope

From *The Way We Live Now* (1875)

Melmotte's electioneering tricks as he tries to be elected to Parliament are, suggests Trollope, symptomatic of the general degeneracy of the age. His analysis demonstrates that the whole of society, the church included, is in thrall to the meretricious values represented by Melmotte.

Roger dined with the Bishop of Elmham that evening, and the same hero was discussed under a different heading. 'He has given £200,' said the Bishop, 'to the Curates' Aid Society. I don't know that a man could spend his money much better than that.'

'Clap-trap!' said Roger, who in his present mood was very bitter.

'The money is not clap-trap, my friend. I presume that the money is really paid.'

'I don't feel at all sure of that.'

'Our collectors for clerical charities are usually stern men, – very ready to make known defalcations on the part of promising subscribers. I think they would take care to get the money during the election.'

'And you think that money got in that way redounds to his credit?'

'Such a gift shows him to be a useful member of society, – and I am always for encouraging useful men.'

'Even though their own objects may be vile and pernicious?'

'There you beg ever so many questions, Mr. Carbury. Mr. Melmotte wishes to get into Parliament, and if there would vote on the side which you at any rate approve. I do not know that his object in that respect is pernicious. And as a seat in Parliament has been a matter of ambition to the best of our countrymen for centuries, I do not know why we should say that it is vile in this man.' Roger frowned and shook his head. 'Of course Mr. Melmotte is not the sort of gentleman whom you have been accustomed to regard as a fitting member for a Conservative constituency. But the country is changing.'

'It's going to the dogs, I think; – about as fast as it can go.'

'We build churches much faster than we used to do.'

'Do we say our prayers in them when we have built them?' asked the Squire. ...

When he got home, he found Father Barham sitting in his library. An accident had lately happened at Father Barham's own establishment. The wind had blown the roof off his cottage; and Roger Carbury, though his affection for the priest was waning, had offered him shelter while the damage was being repaired. Shelter at Carbury Manor was very much more comfortable than the priest's own establishment, even with the roof on, and Father Barham was in clover. Father Barham was reading his own favourite newspaper 'The Surplice', when Roger entered the room. 'Have you seen this, Mr. Carbury?' he said.

'What's this? I am not likely to have seen anything that belongs peculiarly to the "The Surplice".'

'That's the prejudice of what you are pleased to call the Anglican Church. Mr. Melmotte is a convert to our faith. He is a great man, and will perhaps be one of the greatest known on the face of the globe.'

'Melmotte a convert to Romanism! I'll make you a present of him, and thank you to take him; but I don't believe that we've any such good riddance.'

Then Father Barham read a paragraph out of 'The Surplice'. 'Mr. Augustus Melmotte, the great financier and capitalist, has presented a hundred guineas towards the erection of an altar for the new church of St. Fabricius, in Tothill Fields. The donation was accompanied by a letter from Mr. Melmotte's secretary, which leaves but little doubt that the new member for Westminster will be a member, and no inconsiderable member, of the Catholic party in the House, during the next session.'

'That's another dodge, is it?' said Carbury.

'What do you mean by a dodge, Mr. Carbury? Because money is given for a pious object of which you do not happen to approve, must it be a dodge?'

'But, my dear Father Barham, the day before the same great man gave £200 to the Protestant Curates' Aid Society. I have just left the Bishop exulting in this great act of charity.'

'I don't believe a word of it; or it may be parting gift to the Church to which he belonged in his darkness.'

'And you would be really proud of Mr. Melmotte as a convert?'

'I would be proud of the lowest human being that has a soul,' said the priest; 'but of course we are glad to welcome the wealthy and the great.'

'The great! oh dear!'

'A man is great who has made for himself such a position as that of Mr. Melmotte. And when such a one leaves your Church and joins our own, it is a great sign to us that the Truth is prevailing.' Roger Carbury, without another word, took his candle and went to bed.

Mrs Humphry Ward

From *Robert Elsmere* (1888)

This extract – and the one from Newman's *Loss and Gain* on pages 72–73 – illustrates the extremes of religious controversy as represented in the novel: in this, it is the anguish of loss of faith.

The words of St Augustine which he had read to Catherine, taken in a strange new sense, came back to him: "Commend to the keeping of the Truth whatever the Truth hath given thee, and thou shalt lose nothing!"

Was it the summons of Truth which was rending the whole nature in this way?

Robert stood still, and with his hands locked behind him, and his face turned like the face of a blind man toward a world of which it saw nothing, went through a desperate catechism of himself.

"*Do I believe in God?* Surely, surely! 'Though He slay me yet will I trust in Him!' *Do I believe in Christ?* Yes – in the teacher, the martyr, the symbol to us Westerns of all things heavenly and abiding, the image and pledge of the invisible life of the spirit – with all my soul and all my mind!

"*But in the Man-God*, the Word from Eternity – in a wonder-working Christ, in a risen and ascended Jesus, in the living Intercessor and Mediator for the lives of His doomed brethren?"

He waited, conscious that it was the crisis of his history, and there rose in him, as though articulated one by one by an audible voice, words of irrevocable meaning.

"Every human soul in which the voice of God makes itself felt, enjoys, equally with Jesus of Nazareth, the divine worship, and *'miracles do not happen!'*"

It was done. He felt for the moment as Bunyan did after his lesser defeat.

"Now was the battle won, and down fell I as a bird that is shot from the top of a tree into great guilt and fearful despair. Thus getting out of my bed I went moping in the field; but God knows with as heavy a heart as mortal man I think could bear, where for the space of two hours I was like a man bereft of life."

All these years of happy, spiritual certainty, of rejoicing oneness with Christ, to end in this wreck and loss! Was not this indeed "*il gran rifiuto*" – the greatest of which human daring is capable? The lane darkened round him. Not a soul was in sight. The only sounds were the sounds of a gently-breathing nature, sounds of birds and swaying branches and intermittent gusts of air rustling through the gorse and the drifts of last year's leaves in the wood beside him. He moved mechanically onward, and presently, after the first flutter of desolate terror had passed away, with a new inrushing sense which seemed to him a sense of liberty – of infinite expansion.

Suddenly the trees before him thinned, the ground sloped away, and there to the left on the westernmost edge of the hill lay the square stone rectory, its windows open to the evening coolness, a white flutter of pigeons round the dove-cote on the side lawn, the gold of the August wheat in the great corn-field showing against the heavy girdle of oak-wood.

Robert stood gazing at it – the home consecrated by love, by effort, by faith. The high alternations of intellectual and spiritual debate, the strange emerging sense of deliverance, gave way to a most bitter human pang of misery.

"*Oh, God! My wife – my work!*"

Max Beerbohm

'The Feast' from *A Christmas Garland* (1912)

This parody of the writing of Joseph Conrad is also an illustration of the theme of Empire in the Victorian novel. Beerbohm offers insights into an understanding of Conrad by humorously highlighting themes and techniques that pervade his novels. The conflict of the primitive and the civilised and the tragedy of the individual, all set against a lush, exotic background, are familiar characteristics.

The hut in which slept the white man was on a clearing between the forest and the river. Silence, the silence murmurous and unquiet of a tropical night, brooded over the hut that, baked through by the sun, sweated a vapour beneath the cynical light of the stars. Mahamo lay rigid and watchful at the hut's mouth. In his upturned eyes. and along the polished surface of his lean body black and immobile, the stars were reflected, creating an illusion of themselves who are illusions.

The roofs of the congested trees, writhing in some kind of agony private and eternal, made tenebrous and shifty silhouettes against the sky, like shapes cut out of black paper by a maniac who pushes them with his thumb this way and that, irritably, on a concave surface of blue steel. Resin oozed unseen from the upper branches to the trunks swathed in creepers that clutched and interlocked with tendrils venomous, frantic and faint. Down below, by force of habit, the lush herbage went through the farce of growth – that farce old and screaming, whose trite end is decomposition.

Within the hut the form of the white man, corpulent and pale, was covered with a mosquito-net that was itself illusory like everything else, only more so. Flying squadrons of mosquitoes inside its meshes flickered and darted over him, working hard, but keeping silence so as not to excite him from sleep. Cohorts of yellow ants disputed him against cohorts of purple ants, the two kinds slaying one another in thousands. The battle was undecided when suddenly, with so such warning as it gives in some parts of the world, the sun blazed up over the horizon, turning night into day, and the insects vanished back into their camps.

The white man ground his knuckles into the corners of his eyes, emitting that snore final and querulous of a middle-aged man awakened rudely. With a gesture brusque but flaccid he plucked aside the net and peered around. The bales of cotton cloth, the beads, the brass wire, the bottles of rum, had not been spirited away in the night. So far so good. The faithful servant of his employers was now at liberty to care for his own interests. He regarded himself, passing his hands over his skin.

"Hi! Mahamo!" he shouted. "I've been eaten up."

The islander, with one sinuous motion, sprang from the ground, through the mouth of the hut. Then, after a glance, he threw high his hands in thanks to such good and evil spirits as had charge of his concerns. In a tone half of reproach, half of apology, he murmured –

"You white men sometimes say strange things that deceive the heart."

"Reach me that ammonia bottle, d'you hear?" answered the white man. "This is a pretty place you've brought me to!" He took a draught. "Christmas Day, too! Of all the – But I suppose it seems all right to you, you funny blackamoor, to be here on Christmas Day?"

'We are here on the day appointed, Mr. Williams. It is a feast-day of your people?"

Mr. Williams had lain back, with closed eyes, on his mat. Nostalgia was doing duty to him for imagination. He was wafted to a bedroom in Marylebone, where in honour of the Day he lay late dozing, with great contentment; outside a slush of snow in the street, the sound of church-bells; from below a savour of especial cookery.

"Yes," he said, "it's a feast-day of my people."

"Of mine also," said the islander humbly.

"Is it though? But they'll do business first?"

"They must first do that."

"And they'll bring their ivory with them?"

"Every man will bring ivory," answered the islander, with a smile gleaming and wide.

"How soon'll they be here?"

"Has not the sun risen? They are on their way."

"Well, I hope they'll hurry. The sooner we're off this cursed island of yours the better. Take all those things out," Mr. Williams added, pointing to the merchandise, "and arrange them – neatly, mind you!"

In certain circumstances it is right that a man be humoured in trifles. Mahamo, having borne out the merchandise, arranged it very neatly.

While Mr. Williams made his toilet, the sun and the forest, careless of the doings of white and black men alike, waged their warfare implacable and daily. The forest from its inmost depths sent forth perpetually its legions of shadows that fell dead in the instant of exposure to the enemy whose rays heroic and absurd its outposts annihilated. There came from those inilluminable depths the equable rumour of myriads of winged things and crawling things newly roused to the task of killing and being killed. Thence detached itself, little by little, an insidious sound of a drum beaten. This sound drew more near.

Mr. Williams, issuing from the hut, heard it, and stood gaping towards it.

"Is that them?" he asked.

"That is they," the islander murmured, moving away towards the edge of the forest.

Sounds of chanting were a now audible accompaniment to the drum.

"What's that they're singing?" asked Mr. Williams.

"They sing of their business?" said Mahamo.

"Oh!" Mr. Williams was slightly shocked. "I'd have thought they'd be singing of their feast."

"It is of their feast they sing."

It has been stated that Mr. Williams was not imaginative. But a few years of life in climates alien and intemperate had disordered his nerves. There was that in the rhythms of the hymn which made bristle his flesh.

Suddenly, when they were very near, the voices ceased, leaving a legacy of silence more sinister than themselves. And now the black spaces between the trees were relieved by bits of white that were the eyeballs and teeth of Mahamo's brethren.

"It was of their feast, it was of you, they sang," said Mahamo.

"Look here," cried Mr. Williams in his voice of a man not to be trifled with. "Look here, if you've –"

He was silenced by sight of what seemed to be a young sapling sprung up from the ground within a yard of him – a young sapling tremulous, with a root of steel. Then a thread-like shadow skimmed the air, and another spear came impinging the ground within an inch of his feet.

As he turned in his flight he saw the goods so neatly arranged at his orders, and there flashed through him, even in the thick of the spears, the thought that he would be a grave loss to his employers. This – for Mr. Williams was, not less than the goods, of a kind easily replaced – was an illusion. It was the last of Mr. Williams illusions.

4 | Critical approaches

- How have attitudes to the Victorian novel changed?

- Why do some novelists go in and out of fashion?

- In what different ways can a novel be read?

The developing debate on the novel

Novels had had a bad press in the hundred years that preceded Victoria's reign: though Jane Austen had made a spirited and famous defence of the form in *Northanger Abbey* in 1797 (see Introduction), there were a dozen negative comments, thoughtful or contemptuous, for every word of praise the novel got. Even Sir Walter Scott, subsequently idolised as the greatest of all novelists, and the father of the Victorian novel, was snarled at by reviewers early on for using up his genius on such a lowly branch of literature. But attitudes changed and by the end of the Queen's reign in 1901 the novel had established itself as the undisputed leading form in literature – a position it held for a great deal of the 20th century.

The Humanist School: David Cecil and *Early Victorian Novelists*

The critical debate in the 20th century has been less about the status of the novel as a form than about the different perspectives from which it can be approached. Reputations have been made and unmade as novelists have been discovered and attacked (and then abandoned) by different critics and schools of criticism throughout the century. Lord David Cecil, author of *Early Victorian Novelists* (1934) and a very influential critic of the Victorian novel between and after the two World Wars, wrote wisely about re-reading his own work thirty years later:

> It made me realise as never before that criticism is always written in the context established by the literary taste prevalent in its period.
> (Preface, Fontana edition, 1964)

Cecil acknowledged that his own epoch-making book was written, in a sense, in reaction to 'the literary taste prevalent in 1934' – which was, in itself, in reaction against 'the moralistic, insular and philistine aspects of Victorianism'. The young critics of the 1930s, he said, held that 'art had nothing to do with morals', but should be solely concerned with form and style – which they found in 19th-century French fiction rather than in English fiction. They dismissed Dickens and George

Eliot in favour of Flaubert and Proust, novelists who judged fiction in terms of its 'specifically aesthetic qualities'. Cecil, on the other hand, writing in reaction to contemporary taste, established a humanist view of literature. He promoted novelists (for example, Trollope) on the grounds of their 'knowledge of human nature, their creative imagination'. His concern was with the mind of the novelist, which controls the text.

In *Early Victorian Novelists* Cecil rescued various novelists from the neglect into which they had (undeservedly) fallen, and from the contumely of the 'learned and Olympian kind of critic' who 'speaks of them less than of the French or Russian novelists'. He is one of the early critics to give serious attention to the Victorian novel as a form, and to recognise that 'there is one sort of novel before George Eliot and another after her'. From the novelists he chose for his examination, he created a canon which has endured. That Thackeray, Gaskell and Eliot enjoy the esteem they do today is, in part, due to Cecil's perceptions in 1934. The criteria by which he admits them to greatness may sound naive and unsophisticated today, but when he was writing they broke new ground. For Cecil '... the specific mark of a work of art is that it is a "creation", a new, individual and living entity, owing something of its character, no doubt, to its subject and more to the personality of its creator, yet differing from and independent of either. Without this independent vitality the most accomplished portrait remains a photograph ... And the distinguishing, essential qualification of the artist is ... "creative imagination".' It is this quality, he declares, which most distinguishes the Victorian novelists:

> The material of the novelist is the world of human beings and their relations to each other. Then he apprehends and selects in such a way as to create a new world, founded it is true on the real one, and, it may be, elucidating certain aspects of it, but with an independent energy and idiosyncrasy of its own.
> ... [the novelists'] merits are of so superlative a kind, forged in the central heat of the creative imagination, rich in the essential precious stuff from which the art of the novel is made.

On these grounds all the imperfections of the Victorian novel – improbable plots, conventional endings, lack of coherence – are transcended: the genius of the author is all that matters.

▶ Cecil's view that 'the material of the novelist is the world of human beings and their relations to each other' can be called the manifesto of the Humanist School. Do you agree with Cecil that in the novels you have read the novelist creates 'a new world' with its own 'independent energy and idiosyncrasy'?

Cecil's defence of George Eliot

Two chapters of *Early Victorian Novelists* stand out in particular, though for different reasons: that on George Eliot and that on Emily Brontë. George Eliot's reputation had slumped to its lowest point in the 1920s, something Cecil acknowledged ('... her reputation has sustained a more catastrophic slump than any of her contemporaries'). Cecil does a determined job of restoration. His tone, all the same, is apologetic and concessionary. He would place George Eliot ultimately among the great, but at this point, when her reputation has dwindled low, he makes the claim almost defiantly. He concedes most of the weaknesses of which she is accused by contemporary readers (plot construction, setting, character) but points to her 'creative impulse' which, he claims, is 'stimulated by a new sort of inspiration', and insists that she is finally redeemed by her intellect, her 'disciplined generalising intelligence', and her power of analysing 'psychological essentials' and states of mind. This is what distinguishes her from every other Victorian novelist.

Middlemarch, says Cecil firmly, is her masterpiece, and fit to stand as the nearest equivalent to *War and Peace*. In this she is like no other novelist: George Eliot is inspired by what she thought, by ideas. She is concerned with 'how to live and what to think'. Her intention is 'to convey [not] her impressions of life, but her judgements on it'. In her hands 'novels aspire to be a serious major form of art': her books are 'a criticism of life'. And this – and the terms are startling to a modern reader – in spite of the 'dowdiness, ponderousness, and earnestness' of her personal appearance, and the one time reputation of her novels, is what sets her in the same league as the greatest. The rediscovery of George Eliot had begun.

Cecil and *Wuthering Heights*

It is Cecil's view of *Wuthering Heights* which became one of the most widely accepted interpretations, and for generations of readers the obvious one. For a line of subsequent critics, Cecil's influence is clear in the rhapsodic tone which prevails, and in his theories of the inspiration of the writer. Early contemporary critics (Charlotte Brontë is among the first, with her Preface to the novel in 1850) had found the work 'wild, confused, disjointed, and improbable' (*Examiner*, 1848), the 'worst constructed tale that ever was written'. To them Heathcliff was merely 'an incarnation of evil qualities: implacable hate, ingratitude, cruelty, falsehood, selfishness, and revenge', and they had remarked primly '... it is with difficulty that we can prevail upon ourselves to believe in the appearance of such a phenomenon, so near our own dwellings as the summit of a Lancashire or Yorkshire moor'. Cecil, by contrast, discounts the Victorian search for 'realism' and suggests a structure to the novel which is metaphysical.

Wuthering Heights, he insists, was never intended to be the same sort of novel as *Vanity Fair* or *David Copperfield* – Emily Brontë 'stands outside the main current of 19th-century fiction as Blake stands outside the main current of 18th-century poetry'. He sees her as a mystic, and expresses her vision in terms of 'storm and calm'.

> The first [of her principles] is that the whole created cosmos, animate and inanimate, mental and physical alike, is the expression of certain living, spiritual principles: on the one hand what may be called the principle of storm – of the harsh, the ruthless, the wild, the dynamic; and on the other, the principle of calm – the gentle, the merciful, the passive and the tame. Secondly, in spite of their apparent opposition these principles are not conflicting. Either – Emily Brontë does not make clear which she thinks – each is the expression of a single pervading spirit; or they are the component parts of a harmony … Such convictions inevitably set Emily Brontë's view of life in a perspective fundamentally different from that presented by other English novelists. For they do away with these antitheses which are the basis of these novelists' conceptions … [He cites Gaskell and Hardy.] Men and nature to her are equally living, and in just the same way. To her an angry man and an angry sky are not just metaphorically alike, they are actually alike in kind; different manifestations of single spiritual reality.

The 'storm and calm' principle informs Brontë's whole vision of life: in terms of morality right and wrong are irrelevant concepts, there is simply the cosmic scheme of like and unlike. Human emotions and the deepest feelings depend on a sense of affinity, and that 'comes from the fact that they are both expressions of the same spiritual principle'. Hence Catherine Earnshaw's famous declaration of her feelings for Heathcliff: she loves him 'not because he's handsome … but because he's more myself than I am. Whatever our souls are made of, his and mine are the same … My love for Heathcliff resembles the eternal rocks beneath: a source of little visible delight, but necessary. Nelly, I am Heathcliff …'.

Even life and death and the hereafter are explained in terms of the cosmic affinity between souls. As Cecil explains it:

> She does more than believe in the immortality of the soul in the orthodox Christian sense. She believes in the immortality of the soul in this world …

▶ Do you agree with David Cecil that for Emily Brontë right and wrong are irrelevant concepts? Is a moral vision essential for any novelist, or only for those working within the conventions of realism?

The New Criticism: F.R. Leavis and *The Great Tradition*

Cecil's reading of *Wuthering Heights* became an orthodoxy which has survived to the present day, and his influence has been discernible in a line of critics. But other critics who followed disagreed with him profoundly. F.R. Leavis in *The Great Tradition* (1948) takes issue generally with Cecil and the critical school of liberal humanism he represents.

The Great Tradition is not a survey of the novel, but essays on a selection of those novelists who, Leavis thinks, have contributed most to the seriousness of the form, and he limits these – provocatively – to three, George Eliot, Henry James and Joseph Conrad (with respectful notes on notable figures at either end of the 'tradition', Jane Austen and D.H. Lawrence). The 'great tradition' as he identifies it has been the tradition in English fiction of serious moral concern. (Leavis calls the novelists he identifies 'significant in the terms of human awareness they promote: awareness of the possibilities of life'.)

Dickens is left out on the grounds that his 'genius' was that of 'the great entertainer': the adult mind, says Leavis, 'doesn't as a rule find in Dickens a challenge to an unusual and sustained seriousness'. (Leavis was to change his mind about this notorious view, and later collaborated with his wife, Q.D. Leavis, on a famous disclaimer, *Dickens the Novelist* [1970]. But the damage had been done and as a result of *The Great Tradition* Dickens' reputation among the critics was to suffer badly for a generation.) Emily Brontë is excluded because, although a genius, she added nothing to the 'tradition'. And Charlotte Brontë, although she had 'a remarkable talent', has 'no part in the great line of English fiction'.

Leavis was not concerned with the historical dimension of a novel, nor with the conditions under which a novelist worked, nor with the biographical details of the author, only with the text in front of him – and in this he can be said to belong to the New Critics. This was originally an American school of criticism in the 1930s which concentrated simply on the 'words on the page', and insisted that poems and novels be organic and self-contained wholes or structures. The New Criticism was much concerned with aesthetic and technical effects in a work, in its technical organisation, for example, or the creation of character, and the artistic unity which these should produce. And the most important of all the qualities in a work was its moral seriousness.

Leavis and George Eliot

Leavis discerns moral seriousness in abundance in George Eliot, and refers throughout the chapter on her in *The Great Tradition* to her 'moral preoccupations', her 'intense moral seriousness' (which Cecil, he tells us, had dismissed as Puritanism and schoolteacherliness), and this is 'the distinctive quality of her art'. Cecil's approach had been through the intelligence of George Eliot, which almost, he feels, over-rides her failure in imagination: 'Her imagination was quite wide enough to cover the ground explored by a domestic novel ... But it was not wide enough to cover the ground needed for an adequate criticism of life. And her intellect spurred her to attempt such criticism ...' (*Early Victorian Novelists*). Leavis champions her on wider grounds, for her 'radically reverent attitude towards life, a profound seriousness of the kind that is a first condition of any real intelligence, and an interest in human nature that made her a great psychologist'.

Formalism: Dorothy Van Ghent and *The English Novel: Form and Function*

Another name for the New Criticism was 'formalism', and the 'formalistic' critical method was the most influential of all schools in the middle decades of the century. Formalistic criticism is less concerned with art as an expression of social, ethical, psychological or political ideas than with art as a form and involves primarily the close study of the texts themselves. The author is not seen as the central force in the text (as the humanist critic saw him/her) – it is 'the word on the page' which is important.

Imagery, and a study of the patterns of imagery in a novel or poem, is very much associated with formalism, and is seen as part of the structure of the work. One of the most important of the writers involved in this form of critical discourse was Dorothy Van Ghent, an American critic, who in 1953 published *The English Novel: Form and Function* in which she examined the whole nature and purpose of the novel as a form, and looked at a representative selection of novels.

Van Ghent and *Wuthering Heights*

Her analysis of *Wuthering Heights* is famous and, like Cecil's, has become an accepted reading of the novel. It focuses on specific patterns of imagery in the text: the use made of windows, the oppositions between 'outside' and 'inside', and the dualities which exist – the novel is 'a tension between two kinds of reality'.

> The first kind of reality is given to the imagination in the violent figures of Catherine and Heathcliff, portions of the flux of nature, children of rock and heath and tempest, striving to identify themselves as human ... Set over against the wilderness of inhuman reality is the quietly secular, voluntarily limited, safely human reality that we find in the gossipy concourse of Nelly Dean and Lockwood. ... This second kind of reality is found also in the romance of Cathy and Hareton, where books and gentled manners and domestic

charities form a little island of complacence. The tension between these two kinds of reality ... provides at once the content and the form of *Wuthering Heights* ... The form, in short, is the book itself.

Sociological criticism: Arnold Kettle and *Introduction to the English Novel*

Another critical approach which was emerging at the same time was that of the sociological or Marxist school, which held that art's relations with society are vitally important and that it is the task of the critic to investigate these relationships in order to deepen the reader's awareness of the extent to which art is compromised by the circumstances of its production.

The social milieu and how the novelist responds to it are the important questions for the sociological critic. One early and influential critic of this school was Arnold Kettle, who writes very much from a Marxist point of view. In 'The Nineteenth Century' section of his important *Introduction to the English Novel* (1951), he points out that even by the time of Jane Austen at the beginning of the century the industrial revolution was under way. A new and immensely powerful class – that of the industrial capitalists – was in the ascendancy, and this had inevitable consequences for the novel. It was a class that set itself against art; and throughout the century 'honest writers were bound to feel a deep revulsion against the underlying principles and warped relationships of the society they lived in'.

Novelists as critics of society

For this reason, argues Kettle, the great novelists were rebels, sensing and exposing 'the degradation of human existence in Victorian society' and defiantly espousing the art despised by the Gradgrinds and Bounderbys of society. He sees *Wuthering Heights* not in Cecil's transcendental account, outside the boundaries of space and time, nor in Van Ghent's imagistic perspective, but in very concrete terms:

> *Wuthering Heights* is about England in 1847. The people it reveals are not in a never-never land but in Yorkshire. Heathcliff was born not in the pages of Byron, but in a Liverpool slum. The language of Nelly, Joseph and Hareton is the language of Yorkshire people. The story of *Wuthering Heights* is concerned not with love in the abstract but with the passions of living people, with property-ownership, the attraction of social comforts, the arrangement of marriages, the importance of education, the validity of religion, the relations of rich and poor.

He sees the role of the dual narrative, the voices of Lockwood and Nelly ('the two most "normal" people in the book') as being to provide the voice of common sense, and to maintain credibility in a tale of fantasy and make-believe. In the world of Victorian social mobility, class conflict is expressed in Catherine's seduction by the bourgeois glamour of Thrushcross Grange, and Heathcliff's rejection of it. Heathcliff's ambition – 'the triumph of seeing my descendants fairly lord of their estates! My child hiring their children to till their father's lands for wages' – continues the theme. Moreover, Kettle argues, Heathcliff retains sympathy because instinctively the reader recognises a rough moral justice in what he has done to his oppressors and because, though he is inhuman, 'we understand why he is inhuman ... We recognise the very forces which drove him to rebellion for a higher freedom have themselves entrapped him in their own values and determined the nature of his revenge.' He speaks in terms of Heathcliff as the representative of the turbulent rebellious workmen of the 1840s, and reminds the reader of the place of Haworth (where Emily Brontë was writing) in the industrial revolution and its 'attendant social unrest'.

For Arnold Kettle, then, *Wuthering Heights* is 'an expression in the imaginative terms of art of the stresses and tensions and conflicts, personal and spiritual, of nineteenth-century capitalist society'. For him what the novel conveys is:

> [T]his unending struggle, of which the struggle to advance from class society to a higher humanity of a classless world is but an episode ... [I]t is conveyed to us in *Wuthering Heights* precisely because the novel is conceived in actual, concrete, particular terms, because the quality of oppression revealed in the novel is not abstract but concrete, not vague but particular.

The novel is both 'a statement about ... the life of Victorian England, and a statement about life as such'.

▶ What are the essential differences between David Cecil, Dorothy Van Ghent and Arnold Kettle in their approaches to *Wuthering Heights*? How easily could you apply these approaches to other Victorian novels you have read?

Kettle reads all the novels he selects in *Introduction to the English Novel* in the same way. The 'core' of *Oliver Twist* is its consideration of the plight of the poor:

> This pattern is the contrasted relation of the two worlds – the underworld of the workhouse, the funeral parlour, the thieves' kitchen, and the comfortable world of the Brownlows and Maylies ... The power of the book proceeds from the wonderful evocation of the underworld and the engagement of our sympathy on behalf of the inhabitants of that world. The oppression of the poor stems from the

'Board' – 'eight or ten fat gentlemen sitting round a table … The methods of oppression are simple: violence and starvation … The oppressed are degraded and corrupted by their life (plus a little gin) and either become themselves oppressors or else criminals or corpses'.

Proving a similar point about the class struggle, Kettle suggests that in *Vanity Fair* Thackeray's characters, as well as being individuals, are 'types':

Charlie Chaplin on the screen is not an average man … and yet he is unmistakably typical, not just an oddity for all his uniqueness, but somehow more typical of the 'little man', the individual worker in our industrial society, than any little man we actually know … Becky is an unmistakable individual, yet she is everywoman of spirit rebelling against the humiliations forced on her by certain social assumptions. Old Osborne, similarly, is every successful nineteenth-century business man, encased in a gloomy, luxurious ugliness in that big house in Russell Square … Thackeray himself does his best to destroy his picture of the ruling-class world …

And Kettle concludes:

The artistic motive-force of *Vanity Fair* is Thackeray's vision of bourgeois society and of personal relationships engendered by that society. That is what his novel is about.

Viewed from this position, *Middlemarch* is a gravely flawed masterpiece. Its limitations include '[George Eliot's] somewhat static view of society and morality' and her consequent failure to impose an organic unity on the novel. She had intended, Kettle presumes, that the town of Middlemarch should be the unifying factor, but in the event it is not: although by Chapter 11 the town has taken over from Dorothea Brooke as the central character, and the theme, clearly, is how society forces the individual into its own mould, her study of society is finally a failure. The 'subtle movement' of society which George Eliot herself refers to is not caught in the novel:

[The novel's] richness lies in a consideration of individual characters firmly placed in an actual social situation … [But there is] a contradiction between the success of the parts and the relative failure of the whole.

Sociological interpretations of literature (the work of such writers as the Marxist and political critics who interpret literature as a manifestation of the class struggle) continue today. Readings of the Victorian novel in this light include the critical work by Raymond Williams and Terry Eagleton, whose books *The English Novel from Dickens to Hardy* (1970), *The Country and the City* (1973) (by Williams), and *Myths of Power* (1975, 1988) and *Heathcliff and the Great Hunger* (1995) (by Eagleton), have been very influential.

Psychological criticism

Since the ground-breaking interpretation of *Hamlet* in Freudian terms in 1910 by Dr Ernest Jones, a British psychoanalyst, the critical school which attempts to read literature in terms of the unconscious intentions of the author, and the motives of fictitious characters, has gained significant ground, seeming to offer the most appropriate key to the process of art. Psychology offered critics a more precise language with which to discuss the creative process; it enabled the lives of writers to be studied as a way of understanding their work; and it could be used to explain fictitious characters. (These different schools of criticism can and do often overlap, of course. In recent years psychological criticism has sometimes merged with other modes of criticism, such as structuralism and feminist criticism [see below, pages 102–103 and 100–101]).

The Victorian novel has come in for its fair share of attention from psychological criticism. *Great Expectations*, for example, has been interpreted in the light of Freud's theories. In a chapter from *The Dickens Theatre* (1965), Robert Garis interprets Pip as lacking in 'libido':

> ... [I]f we should stop to think about the curious emptiness of Pip's response to Biddy's marriage, it would immediately occur to us that the response is not in the least surprising, since we have known all along that Pip is like that, that something is missing in him ... We have known from the beginning of the novel that what is missing from Pip's life is any free expression of libido, and that it is missing because it is held in contempt and horror by the ideals of the civilisation within which Pip tries to make a life for himself. It must have been for this reason that Dickens was drawn to the characterisation, as he was earlier drawn to Arthur Clennam (in *Little Dorrit*) and was later to Eugene Wrayburn (*Our Mutual Friend*). Although Pip is, beneath the surface of the novel, known to us as 'the man without will, the man who cannot act', yet on the surface of the novel he is defined as 'the man who wanted and acted wrongly'.
>
> (Quoted in *Great Expectations*, Icon Critical Guides, 1998)

Using a similar approach, another critical reading suggests the function of Orlick in the novel as Pip's 'double': '... [T]here is a peculiar parallel between the careers of the two characters', and Orlick seems to 'present a parody of Pip's upward progress through the novel, as though he were in competitive pursuit of some obscene great expectations of his own.' (ibid)

A third reading is based on the theories of Freud's French disciple, Lacan, and explores Pip's attempt 'to find some interpretation of an individual self into social life':

> Throughout most of the narrative Pip mistakes 'otherness' for himself, remoulding people and events in order to have them conform to his private fantasy. This egoism involves the continual rejection of all antipathetic elements. So, in order to become a gentleman, Pip must repress the memory of the association with Magwitch. He also rejects others, of course, including his bogus benefactor, Pumblechook, and the frightening Orlick, not to mention Joe and the life of the forge. Pip therefore achieves totality and unity of self only at the cost of excluding fundamental parts of himself.
>
> (ibid)

Given the myths which have grown up round *Wuthering Heights*, it is predictable that the psychological critics should have had a field day with this text. In fact, it has attracted more attention in this field than almost any other Victorian novel. Emily Brontë has been psychoanalysed, her characters dissected in terms of their desires and dreams (both terms in the discourse of Freud), the concern of the structuralist school (see below, pages 102–103) with kinship stuctures and taboos has been examined. Even the post-structuralist school (see below, page 103), which seeks to examine the subconscious in the text rather than in the author, is represented in readings of the novel. Throughout the century critics have explored the sexual implications of the novel, especially in Heathcliff, whether these were conscious or unconscious in the author's mind (even Charlotte Brontë implies them in her 1850 Preface). It was not until much later that these implications were expressed in directly Freudian terms: one analysis of 1962 speaks of Heathcliff as 'the source of psychic energy, the seat of the instincts (particularly sex and death ... pure sexual force ...' (quoted in *Wuthering Heights*, Icon Critical Guides, 1998), but the Freudian critics since have found evidence of the Oedipal complex, and themes of repression, incest, infanticide and sadism. Dreams and taboos have been rich fields of investigation; and feminist critics have been vigorous in their use of Freudian theory.

Feminist criticism

Feminist criticism, which has flourished since the late 1960s, emphasises culturally determined gender differences in the interpretation of literary texts. Generally speaking, the early feminist critics such as Kate Millett, Ellen Moers and Elaine Showalter highlighted men's attitudes to women, and focused on the history of male dominance and oppression. A later strand looks for evidence of essential femaleness in the textual discourse. This later feminist school includes French critics like Helene Cixous (for example, 'The Laugh of Medusa' in *New French Feminisms*, 1980) and Julia Kristeva (*Revolution in Poetic Language*, 1984), and in the field of the Victorian novel, such critics as Patsy Stoneman, Margaret Homans and Kate Flint. This form of criticism frequently overlaps with other schools already considered – Freudian, psychological, sociological – and even more with modern schools such as structuralism and poststructuralism.

The Victorian novel has, again, been a focus for this mode of critical discourse, though some texts more than others. *Jane Eyre*, *Villette* and *Shirley*, for instance, are much more obviously about 'the woman question' than novels such as *Barchester Towers* or *The Egoist*; but in more recent readings *Wuthering Heights*, for example, has been seen as a positive text for women. Ellen Moers, a distinguished early feminist critic, musing in 1976 about the love between Heathcliff and Cathy, says:

> The puzzles of *Wuthering Heights* may be best resolved if the novel is read as a statement of a very serious kind about a girl's childhood and the adult woman's tragic yearning to return to it. Catherine's impossible love for Heathcliff becomes comprehensible as a pre-adolescent (but not pre-sexual) love modelled after the sister-brother relationship. The gratuitous cruelties of the novel are thus justified as realistic attributes of the nursery world – and as frankly joyous memories of childhood eroticism.
>
> (*Literary Women*)

Later, in their seminal contribution to feminist critical ideology, *The Madwoman in the Attic*, Gilbert and Gubar observe:

> Critics never comment on this point, but the truth is that Catherine is pregnant during both the kitchen scene and the mad scene, and her death occurs at the time of (and ostensibly because of) her 'confinement'. In the light of this her anorexia, her madness, and her masochism become even more fearsomely meaningful. Certainly, for instance, the distorted body that the anorexic imagines for herself is

analogous to the distorted body that the pregnant woman must really confront.

(Quoted in *Wuthering Heights*, Icon Critical Guides, 1998)

Feminist critics do not, of course, automatically see Heathcliff as the central character!

▶ Compare the different interpretations of *Wuthering Heights* summarised so far in this section. Do you find some of them more convincing than others? If so, why?

Feminist readings of male-authored novels suggest other emphases than the traditional ones. Recent explorations of *Great Expectations*, such as Catherine Waters' *Dickens and the Politics of the Family*, see Pip's story as 'the record of mid-Victorian anxieties about male identity in a period of rapid industrial change and rampant industrialisation', and Miss Havisham as a 'bizarre example of maternal deviance':

> As the emblem of faded virginity, Miss Havisham forms the focus for a cluster of ideas associated with sterility, solitude, decay and death in the novel. She has reached the third biological stage of womanhood defined in Victorian medical discourse, the 'climacteric', or menopause, without having experienced the stage most crucial in the formation of female subjectivity: pregnancy. Her aging female body, like the 'wilderness of empty corks'... scattered in the disused brewery-yard surrounding the house, suggests barrenness and senescence ...
>
> (Quoted in *Great Expectations*, Icon Critical Guides, 1998)

Post-colonial criticism

Post-colonial criticism has made a significant contribution to critical discourse in the years following the granting of independence to the colonies that made up the British Empire and then the Commonwealth, and is now an important school of criticism. The writing to which post-colonial theory was first applied was the literature produced in these countries, but it is now applied to colonial representation generally. In the criticism of the Victorian novel the main function of this school has been to deconstruct texts in which the representation of colonial subjects is explicitly or implicitly depicted.

Post-colonial criticism explores covert imperial issues, such as slavery or appropriation, as they appear in novels like *Wuthering Heights* and *Jane Eyre*; and where former colonies like Australia and Canada form a significant part of the novels by, say, Dickens and Gaskell. The school also deconstructs the texts which refer to actual colonial material or use the colonial as a site for the exploration of the exotic, the alien, the unknown (as in the novels of, for example, Wilkie Collins, Conrad, Rider Haggard and Kipling).

A very important landmark in post-colonial criticism was the appearance of Edward W. Said's *Orientalism* in 1978 (and later his *Culture and Imperialism*, published in 1993). This foregrounds the 'imperialist' and 'colonialist' dimensions of a selection of texts. Said emphasises the importance of Australia in *Great Expectations*, for example, as the source of Pip's 'great expectations', in that it is the penal colony to which Magwitch is transported, or as the location for Pip's later career as a Victorian businessman.

In *Wuthering Heights*, too, the reader is constantly made aware of Britain's imperialist past: post-colonial critics have identified Heathcliff, for example, as a Creole or a half-caste, an oppressed alien who is found in Liverpool, the port of the slave-trade, or see him as 'an image of the famished Irish immigrant' (Eagleton) after the Potato Famine.

In an important book of 1996, *Imperialism at Home: Race and Victorian Women's Fiction*, Susan Meyer links the issues of race and gender in her examination of *Wuthering Heights*:

> Emily Brontë makes an extended critique of British imperialism. She does this in part by exploring what would happen if the suppressed power of the 'savage' outsiders were unleashed … [She] invokes the metaphorical link between white women and people of non-white races as she explores energies of resistance to the existing social structure.
> (Quoted in *Wuthering Heights*, Icon Critical Guides, 1998)

Gayatri Chakravorty Spivak illuminatingly discusses *Jane Eyre* and Jean Rhys's *The Wide Sargasso Sea* in 'Three Women's Texts and a Critique of Imperialism' (*Critical Inquiry*, 1985), and Paul Sharrad gives a colonialist reading of *Oliver Twist* in 'Speaking the Unspeakable' (*De-scribing Empire*, 1994).

Other recent critical approaches

In the last thirty years, literary criticism has developed dramatically in the ways suggested by the 'formalistic' approach of the 1930s and 1940s, in that critical attention focuses on language and the text: how a message is communicated as much as what the message is.

Structuralism

Structuralism is based on communications theory and is a discipline that embraces a range of other disciplines. Claud Levi-Strauss, who 'invented' it, was not a literary critic but a social anthropologist, and the very word 'structuralism' derives from the modern linguistics of Saussure and Chomsky. In literary criticism the method is used to uncover structural relationships between different elements in the text. Previous schools of criticism have seen the author as central to a reading of the text; however, for critics in the structuralist school (and few contemporary critics are unaffected) it is the systems of meaning which control, rather than being controlled by, the imagination of the writer.

'Post-structuralism' is a term that can refer to any recent trends in criticism, but is frequently used as a synonym for 'deconstruction'.

Deconstruction

The other strand in contemporary criticism, and closely linked to structuralism, is 'deconstruction', a term coined by the French philosopher Jacques Derrida. Since the late 1960s it has come to designate the criticism practised by eminent American critics such as J. Hillis Miller or the British novelist and critic David Lodge. Like structuralism it is based on a reliance on the language of the text for deciphering meaning. Deconstruction (which suggests analysis rather than destruction) raises the question whether any authoritative single 'meaning' is actually discernible in a given text: texts are made up of language, and are therefore full of ambiguity and incoherence. The 'truth' of a text must always be relative, dependent on socially endorsed value judgements; literary criticism is a philosophical exploration of language and how it is used to investigate the possibilities of meaning. The 'author' is irrelevant.

So Hillis Miller, writing about *Wuthering Heights* and dismissing all previous readings, declares that:

> [My] argument is that the best readings will be the ones which best account for the homogeneity of the text, its presentation of a definite group of possible meanings which are systematically interconnected, determined by the text but logically incompatible ... the secret truth about *Wuthering Heights* ... is that there is no secret truth.
> (Quoted in *Wuthering Heights*, Icon Critical Guides, 1998)

A unified single meaning is impossible, in fact.

Speaking of another Victorian novel in this context, Allen Samuels points out in an essay on *Hard Times*, that the novel is a text and therefore made up of language 'which is an endless system of signs and signifiers', and therefore 'full of incoherences, indecisions, ambiguities ...'. So the novel, although it apparently has a clear object in view, which is 'to show the opposition of fact and fancy, in which the author declares his preference for the one against the other ...' in fact demonstrates '... at the textual, linguistic level that these oppositions cannot be consistently sustained, and they begin to lose their distinction from one another ...' ('Hard Times' in *Critics' Debate*).

To illustrate this he quotes at length the example picked up by the critic Stephen Connor of Mrs Sparsit's staircase:

> Mrs Sparsit was not a poetical woman; but she took an idea, in the nature of an allegorical fancy, into her head ... She erected in her mind a mighty Staircase, with a dark pit of shame and ruin at the bottom, and down the stairs, from day to day and hour to hour, she saw Louisa coming ...

Samuels concurs with Connor's reading that Dickens here seems to be calling in question his object in the novel. In giving Mrs Sparsit this imaginative leap of fancy in her use of metaphor (one which Dickens borrows back and uses himself as the author in subsequent chapters), Dickens is using Fancy to attack Fact. Samuels quotes the unconscious complicity between Dickens' language and Mrs Sparsit's '[as] a sign of a more deeply rooted association between the dominant metaphorical mode of signification it condemns in Gradgrind and the party of Fact ... Metaphor is repeatedly used to discredit metaphor as Dickens mounts a systematic assault on systematic thought.' (*Critics' Debate*)

In other words Dickens is guilty of having it both ways: on the one hand, he condemns Mrs Sparsit and 'the party of Fact' for trying to eliminate imagination from the minds and lives of the people of Coketown and thus stunting the emotions of people like Louisa; on the other hand, he allows Mrs Sparsit to have an 'allegorical fancy' (produced by her own imagination) which he then uses as a metaphor for Louisa's downfall.

Samuels comments on 'the curious nature, as it appears to the deconstructionist reading, of this identification of character and author'. He goes on to quote Connor's unease that 'the ironic distance between author and character is abandoned ... the complicity is to see Dickens' control of metaphor as no less coercive than Mrs Sparsit's'. But, since the theme of the book as a whole is the way in which metaphors are used for control and manipulation, then the appeal to Fancy is here undermined.

▶ What arguments could be put forward both in support of, and against, the idea that 'the author is irrelevant' in making a critical response to a Victorian novel?

The place of parody

A penetrating light can be shed on the role and significance of critical theory by study of the parodies to which it gives rise: this mode, far from trivialising the practice, can sometimes bring sharply into focus the key principles of the school of criticism targeted.

David Lodge and *Nice Work*

This mode of approaching literary criticism is seen in David Lodge's novel, *Nice Work* (1988). One of the central characters, Dr Robyn Penrose, is a young university lecturer whose research is on the Victorian industrial novel, and whose passion is contemporary critical theory. In her professional life she writes books on 'the image of women in 19th-century fiction', and teaches Victorian Literature and Women's Studies. Her courses include novels like *Hard Times*, *Wuthering Heights*, *North and South* and *Daniel Deronda*, which she deconstructs from a feminist critical position and in the context of Derrida and the post-structuralists:

> It is interesting how many of the industrial novels were written by women. In their work, the ideological contradictions of the middle-class liberal humanist attitude to the Industrial Revolution take on a specifically sexual character ... The most commonplace metonymic index of industry – the factory chimney – is also metaphorically a phallic symbol.

But she finds that her way of seeing the literary text is straying into her private life too (the novel could be seen in a way as a postmodern re-run of *North and South*). In an experiment between the university and industry, she is assigned to Vic Wilcox as a 'shadow'; and, in the relationship which develops between university lecturer and local factory manager, town and gown find things to learn from each other. Vic Wilcox, in particular, sceptical as he has been about the value to society of Robyn's ideals, comes to learn that 'detracting the hermeneutic code from the proairetic code, the cultural from the symbolic', and discussions of Lacan's psychoanalytic theory, are not the only values in Robyn's life and that semiotics and Saussure have useful things to say to him too. He comes to respond to the humanising influence of Tennyson, and is learning through literature some of the lessons that Gaskell was urging in *North and South*.

▶ Do you think that literary parody such as *Nice Work* can have both a critical and a creative validity?

20th-century writers writing back

The technique known as 'writing back', a mode of commentary on the Victorian novel and on the culture and society which produced it, has become increasingly popular since the 1960s. Fiction of this kind offers a valuable and illuminating commentary on the theory of the Victorian novel. It could thus be described as a self-conscious, postmodern mode, where the central subject of the novel is the novel itself.

This is true of three famous 20th-century novels: John Fowles' *The French Lieutenant's Woman* (1969), David Lodge's *Nice Work* (1988) and A.S. Byatt's *Possession* (1990). Fowles' novel is set in the 1860s, but the 20th-century narrator, who knows what happened later to novel writing in the hands of Alain Robbe-Grillet and Roland Barthes, presents the hero Charles as a modern figure caught up in history. Lodge's *Nice Work* (already discussed on page 105) is set in the 1980s in Mrs Thatcher's Britain where the power of the unions is being aggressively challenged (for instance during the Miners' Strike of 1984), but is consciously modelled on Gaskell's *North and South*. A.S. Byatt's *Possession* – a detective novel, a campus novel and a 'romance' – moves back and forth between the 1850s and the world of the modern university. All the novels in their different ways, explore the theories and conventions which characterised and – to a 20th-century eye – constrained the Victorian novel.

Two aspects in particular of Victorian usage reappear in each of the texts: questions of 'character', and the question of closure, the sense of an ending.

Character

In *The French Lieutenant's Woman*, John Fowles breaks off in Chapter 13 to discuss with the reader the way in which a fictional character is able to achieve a certain autonomy, and take on a life independent of his creator. The novelist, argues Fowles, is only God in the theological sense that his creations have free will and freedom. A genuinely created character, he claims, 'must be independent of its creator ... it is only when our characters begin to disobey us that they begin to live'. And so Charles acts, at various points of the novel, independently of his creator's expectations of how a hero in a Victorian novel should act. As Fowles puts it:

> ... the idea seemed to come clearly from Charles, not myself. It is not only that he has begun to gain an autonomy; I must respect it, and disrespect all my quasi-divine plans for him if I wish him to be real.

Characters are not, he insists, puppets who will respond to the novelist's pulling on the right strings.

Robyn Penrose, one of the central characters in David Lodge's *Nice Work*, is a lecturer in English Literature. She 'holds that "character" is a bourgeois myth, an illusion created to reinforce the ideology of capitalism', and her lectures on the Victorian novel are based on contemporary theory: 'Every text is a product of intertextuality, a tissue of allusions to and citations of other texts.' Lodge, however, acting on a model provided by Gaskell's *North and South*, comments that:

> ... she seems to have ordinary feelings, ambitions, desires, to suffer anxieties, frustrations, fears, like anyone else ... I shall therefore take the liberty of treating her as a character.

▶ Compare Fowles' view of the relationship between a novelist and his characters with that of Thackeray in *Vanity Fair* (see page 61), and with that of David Lodge in *Nice Work*. In what ways do you think it is possible to talk about a character in a novel as 'real'? How explicit do other novelists you have read make their relationship to their characters?

In *Possession* A.S. Byatt writes a serious commentary on various forms of Victorian literature, and she too questions the novel's conventions about character. Her two 20th-century protagonists, Roland and Maud, are specialists in Victorian poetry: together they solve a mystery which they discover hangs over the poets on whom their professional research is based, Randolph Ash and Christabel LaMotte. They do this by an analysis of their poems, letters, diaries, fiction, etc. It is, of course, Byatt herself who writes the 'Victorian' literature in which the secret finally lies, and her text uses several of the characteristics of the traditional Victorian novel – coincidence, melodrama and character – though with intermittent commentary from the contemporary voices of Roland and Maud:

> We are very knowing ... about how there isn't a unitary ego – how we're made up of conflicting, interacting systems of things. ... We know we are driven by desire, but we can't see it as they did, can we? We never say the word love, do we – we know it's a suspect ideological construct – especially Romantic Love – so we have to make a real effort of imagination to know what it felt like to be them.

Closure

The ending, or closure, of the novel was always a problem for the Victorian novelist, and Byatt chooses the traditional, formulaic ending for *Possession*. In the last chapter, the two researchers fall in love, and face an uncertain future together (in 1990, the year in which the contemporary part of the novel is set, marriage and togetherness are not necessarily the given answer). But the future is positive:

> In the morning, the whole world had a strange new smell ... of
> shredded leaves and oozing resin .... It was the smell of death and
> destruction and it smelt fresh and lively and hopeful.

David Lodge also grappled conscientiously with the question of closure, and in *Nice Work* selected another from the traditional list of endings open to the Victorian novelist. Neither marriage, nor even commitment, can be the answer here, but the problems of the reformed factory boss, Vic Wilcox, are resolved (as they had been for Thornton in Gaskell's *North and South*) by an unexpected legacy to Robyn Penrose. John Fowles famously debated the question of closure in *The French Lieutenant's Woman* and offered the reader three possible conclusions: the traditional 'happy' Victorian ending of duty and marriage, an inconclusive ending where Charles is left in a train 'for eternity on his way to London' and the postmodern ending which finally concludes the novel.

Finally, reference to this as 'postmodern' should not make the modern reader forget that Victorian novelists themselves had grappled with the problem of alternative endings. Both Dickens in *Great Expectations* and Hardy in *The Return of the Native* had produced revised and significantly differing conclusions; and Charlotte Brontë had left the final chapter of *Villette* deliberately unresolved.

Assignments

1 What difficulties does closure pose for a novelist? Look at the endings of two or more novels and compare their functions: are they designed either to resolve the main issues of the novel or just to tie up all the loose ends, or do they bring the story to a more open (ambiguous) ending? How far does an ending modify your view of the novel as a whole?

2 Thackeray subtitled *Vanity Fair* 'A novel without a hero'; Hardy subtitled *Tess of the d'Urbervilles* 'A pure woman'; one of the most influential critics of the Victorian novel, Mario Praz, wrote a book called *The Hero in Eclipse*. Explore further the implicit and explicit attitudes to women revealed in the Victorian novel: what new perspectives are opened up for you by a specifically feminist reading of the Victorian novel?

3 What significance do the colonies, or ideas of Empire or Englishness have in any two or more of the Victorian novels you have studied?

5 | How to write about the Victorian novel

Since the Victorian age belongs to a time which is now two centuries away, events and ways of thinking which were once common currency will become progressively less familiar. It will become the more important to be able to place a novel in its context by showing at least some knowledge of incidents and cultural conditions at the time of its composition. It would be impossible today, for example, to read a novel like *Sybil* (1845), *Mary Barton* (1848) or *Hard Times* (1854), without placing the text in the context of the Industrial Revolution. Between 1750 and 1850, this transformed Britain from an agricultural to an industrial economy, but polarised society into what Disraeli (in *Sybil*) called the Two Nations, the rich and the poor.

Parallel texts

Different novelists, as already discussed, use different methods with similar ends: those writing on how Britain responded to the new culture of industrialism were rarely disengaged from their subject, and wrote with a common aim – to call for an end to the abuses in the system.

Other themes can be traced in other novelists, and to identify a theme in one is an aid to identifying it in another. The theme of youthful development, for instance, is readily discerned in a similar novel once it has been identified in a first. Once you have watched the development of *Arthur Pendennis* in Thackeray's novel, you will bring a more developed understanding to your reading (and writing) of *David Copperfield*. These two novels appeared simultaneously in serial form, and both record a young man's education, his successive love affairs, his final marriage to the 'right' woman, and his adoption of authorship as a career.

A familiar theme in the Victorian novel is sometimes seen as the conflict between past and present, between progress and tradition; and novels as apparently far apart in time and technique as *Middlemarch*, *The Warden* and *Tess of the d'Urbervilles* can all be seen to explore this central concern of the 19th century.

▶ On your own, or working with others, draw up a list of all the Victorian novels with which you are familiar. Apart from their primary themes what other topics or issues do they explore? By identifying these secondary themes you may well be able to draw useful comparisons between novels that, at first sight, do not appear to have very much in common.

David Cecil's remark that 'criticism is always written in the context established by the literary taste prevalent in its period' (see Part 4: Critical approaches, page 89), is a warning to those writing on the Victorian novel today that any response is culturally conditioned. The way people are thinking about other issues in society can radically affect how literary texts such as novels are received. Questions of gender, class and politics can shape a reader's response in ways never intended or anticipated by the author. But, always, your personal response, based on a thoughtful reading, is an important first step before the adopting of any particular stance or school.

What kind of a novel is it?

The different kinds of novels are likely, of course, to overlap. The novel of youthful development (the *Bildungsroman*), say, will very possibly contain many of the elements of the novel of domestic life, the novel of religious debate, the political novel, or novels recording other categories of human thought or mental and physical activity. And novels now being re-read in the light of new critical theory could be seen as belonging simultaneously to different genres as different critical approaches (for example, feminist or post-colonial) suggest new understandings of a text.

Nonetheless, various obvious kinds of novel can be seen as belonging to the Victorian period, which can be more readily appreciated when they are read in the context of the culture of the time. And no doubt additional genres and sub-genres will be identified by different readers.

The *Bildungsroman*, however, is one significant genre throughout the period, including a variety of novels from *Jane Eyre* (1847) to *The Way of All Flesh* (1903), and beyond. Newman's novel, *Loss and Gain* (1848), is a record of the religious turmoil which convulsed the country after the Oxford Movement, but it is also the story of how young Charles Reding found answers to the questions which tormented him from youth to early manhood. *Mary Barton* (1848) could well be classed as this kind of novel of development, but it is also, obviously, an industrial novel which documents the changes felt by one particular family as society moved from a rural to an urban economy.

So, in writing about any novel written in the first twenty years of the Victorian period, ask yourself how far it set out to document outward events which were changing society, and how these affected the lives of individuals. How far, at the same time, were the interior movements of mind (the psychological development of the characters) also recorded?

The novel written to express thoughts and ideas more than exterior incident became a force after the middle of the century in the work of novelists like George

Eliot. All her novels, but particularly *Middlemarch* (1871–1872) and *Daniel Deronda* (1876), invited her readers to think about the nature of society itself as well as about the histories of the individuals who make it up. (The sub-title of *Middlemarch*, *A Study of Provincial Life*, is illuminating here.) The novels of Thomas Hardy provocatively goaded the reading public, challenging many received opinions and forcing reassessment of conventional Victorian thinking. And in the work of George Meredith, the novel became a vehicle in which to explore, in the most poetic form yet found in fiction, all his different theories and philosophies. (See Part 1, pages 42–43.)

▶ Re-read the previous paragraph, putting all the verbs into the present tense. When you write about the Victorian novel, what difference does it make to distinguish between the audience that first read the book and the audience that reads it in the the 21st century?

It is important for you to be aware what characterises the novel at these successive phases of its development, and of the overlap between these phases.

As with a text of any date, the first thing to establish after a reading of a novel is how far you can tell what the author intended as the themes or ideas underlying the story, and what response he/she hoped to provoke in the reader. Charlotte Brontë's novel *Shirley* certainly had things to say about the effects of the Industrial Revolution; did *Jane Eyre* address other themes so openly? Did the author have a particular audience in mind? Is there a Preface or Introduction to the novel, written by the author, and setting out what the novel was meant to do? (Sometimes authors wrote such prefaces to the second or later editions of the book, if they felt that original readers and critics had not fully grasped what they had been trying to say.)

You will also want to decide how the author sets about manipulating this response, and what are the techniques being employed to this end. And you will find that one important means is to establish the authorial tone prevalent in the novel. Thackeray, for instance, frequently adopts the tone and persona of a relaxed, urbane, sophisticated man about town, in conversation with a friend; and Trollope is similar. But different novelists adopt different guises, sometimes according to their intention in the novel.

Identifying the author's aims

In the industrial novel, for example, where the intention may be to shock, the tone of the narrative can be passionate. In *Mary Barton*, Elizabeth Gaskell, having seen at first hand the squalor and degradation of the Manchester working class, urgently wishes to communicate them to the reader, who is frequently addressed directly:

> [B]efore you blame too harshly this use [of opium] ... try a hopeless life, with daily cravings of the body for food ... Would you not be glad to forget life, and its burdens? And opium gives forgetfulness for a time. It is true they who purchase it pay dearly for their oblivion; but can you expect the uneducated to count the cost ...? Have you taught them the science of consequences?

She adopts the voice of a concerned, social commentator, setting out to unsettle her complacent readers with the rhetorical questions she poses. Gaskell's intention is to inform the reader as directly as possible of the price in human terms of the prosperity of the nation. Her techniques to bring home to the ignorant middle class readers (themselves 'uneducated' about the realities of working class life) the desperate plight of their neighbours include detailed description of the locale of industrial Lancashire and its inhabitants. Dialogue, too, is regularly expressed in the local dialect (see Part 1, page 24). She intends to shock and to instruct the reader, whose sympathy she takes for granted – she speaks as one humanitarian to another, assuming that once she shares her knowledge with the rest of the world, the problems of society can be resolved.

Disraeli's tone in *Sybil*, on the other hand, is quite different. His material, broadly speaking, may be similar (see pages 24–26), but his intentions are different and he selects quite other techniques, which illustrate the diversity of approaches in the Victorian novel. Here the author is much more detached from his material. Disraeli's intention is as much to promote his own interests as to express his compassion for the poor: his solution to the problems he describes is, he suggests, in the hands of his own pressure group in the Conservative party, Young England.

The tone adopted by the narrator is that of a confident and ambitious young politician. Disraeli draws both characters and plot from melodrama and the dialogue is often as stagy as the dramatis personae – '"Unmannerly churl!" exclaimed Sybil, starting in her chair, her eye flashing lightning, her distended nostril quivering with scorn'. However, it can also express a serious message with both wit and panache.

One of his most successful techniques is the juxtapositioning of different elements in the novel, as in, for example, the opening chapters, which highlight the similarities between the betting activities in the Jockey Club on Derby Day, and the jockeying for position in Parliament as the government of the day is about to collapse. And the boredom of the idle rich, paralysed with *ennui* on their estates and in their stately homes, is contrasted starkly with the squalor and destitution of the slums in a small rural town in the north of England. The whole novel is made up of contrasts like this, part of Disraeli's technique to illustrate his subtitle, *The Two Nations*.

Hard Times offers a third example of the different modes of approach used by the Victorian novelist to explore a similar topic. While Elizabeth Gaskell earnestly uses photographic realism, and emphasises background and characters, and while Disraeli turns to the figures and incidents of melodrama, Dickens employs a whole gallery of different characters, ranging from the grotesque to the sentimental, to make a serious attack on the whole of contemporary culture.

Gaskell believes in the power of well-thinking individuals to change society, and Disraeli's answer lies in the reform of the aristocracy, but Dickens has no ready solution to the problems of society (see Part 1, pages 37–40). His aims in *Hard Times*, and the techniques he uses, are different from the other novelists: he attacks the whole hard Utilitarian philosophy of aggressive money-making and power-seeking, and his technique is to embody the principles of economic individualism in caricatured figures like Thomas Gradgrind and Joseph Bounderby, whose very names are a signpost to their function in the novel. These are all points you, as a reader, must weigh up. It is the cartoon figure of Sleary, the circus owner, who formulates in the last chapter the truth that Dickens is preaching:

> '... There ith a love in the world, not all Thelf-interetht after all, but thomething very different ... it hath a way of ith own of calculating or not calculating, which thomehow or another ith at leatht ath hard to give a name to, ath the wayth of the dogth ith!'

The intentions of other novelists, which may be less obviously pointed than those of authors writing a direct exposé of the evils of industrialism, should also be examined: intentions, tone and technique often overlap with those of more **didactic** novels, and the reader is as frequently asked to make an evaluation or judgement. Social and moral analysis are constantly required of the reader of any Victorian novel, and those writing on the Brontës, George Eliot or Hardy, or on other Dickens novels, will find that the response looked for is regularly one of moral discrimination.

Plot and characterisation

For E.M. Forster, writing in the immediate wake of the Victorian novel, 'the backbone of a novel has to be a story ... the fundamental aspect without which it could not exist', and 'the highest common factor to all novels' (*Aspects of the Novel*) – and certainly it is the basis of all Victorian novels. The story is not the sole requirement of a plot, but it is constant – the answer to the reader's demand 'And then? ... and then?'

But it also happens that the plot itself is of less importance in the novel than the other elements which make it up: the plot provides the necessary framework round which the novelist can organise his/her material, and has a technical function. It is simply a device by which the author drives home the message. The plot in *Jane Eyre*, for example, is less important to Charlotte Brontë's intentions than what it demonstrates about Jane's personality and the author's world-view, and it exists for this purpose; and the plot of *Great Expectations* is only a small part of Dickens' plan for the novel.

▶ In writing about the Victorian novel it may be important to distinguish between plot and story. Look at the way the plot works in any two novels you have read: can you show exactly how the plot acts as a framework in each book? Is the degree of coincidence, for example, acceptable or does it stretch your credulity too far? How does a novelist like Thomas Hardy link his ideas about Fate to the mechanics of his plots?

Another device is the use of character, and one for which the Victorian novel was renowned. The creation of 'realistic', 'rounded' characters (like Jane Eyre and Pip) and intentionally 'flat' characters (like, say, St John Rivers, or Mr Pumblechook) is a much discussed feature of the Victorian novel. A variation on this familiar use of the device is the use of the deliberately diagrammatic figures, as in *Hard Times*: Gradgrind and Bounderby complement each other; characters such as Sissy and Stephen Blackpool contrast with them.

▶ In planning to write about any novel it can be essential to think about all the characters in their relationships with each other. Choose any one Victorian novel and list ALL the characters in it (the sheer number in a Dickens novel can be illuminating). Then show, in diagrammatic form, how they relate to each other. Is there a central character around whom both the action and all the characters revolve? Can you decide, from this diagram, whether the plot or the inter-relationships between characters determines your response to the novel as you study it? If the narrator is one of the characters (not an omniscient narrator) how significantly is he or she placed in your diagram?

Speech

One device by which the reader comes to recognise (and, in a long novel, to remember) any character is speech. Again, Mr Pumblechook from *Great Expectations* is an obvious example, with his obsequious 'May I, Sir?' as he forces his unwelcome handshakes on Pip. This technique is also used with great success by Elizabeth Gaskell or Charlotte Yonge, for whom it is an important feature. The speech patterns, and (in the case of Gaskell in particular) the dialect are prominent signifiers here, and are part of the author's aim for verisimilitude.

This is never, however, Dickens' prime intention: 'reality' for him is something more than surface appearances, and the discourse of his characters expresses truths about humanity at large and Dickens' own world view as much as about, for example, individuals like Joe Gargery and Abel Magwitch in *Great Expectations*.

▶ Contrast the way in which writers like Emily Brontë or Elizabeth Gaskell use Yorkshire or Lancashire dialect in their novels with the way that Dickens presents, say, cockney accents in *The Pickwick Papers* (Sam Weller, for instance). How far does this use of dialect and accent condition your response to the characters?

Locale

The use of locale, or setting, is another device by which the novelist communicates his/her message to the reader. Disraeli's description of the foul industrial slum, Wodgate, juxtaposed with the London clubs of the effete young noblemen, and the frigid sterility of Lord Marney's stately home, is an example in *Sybil*. Dickens' use of the fog-bound City of London in the opening chapter of *Bleak House*, or of the Marshalsea Prison and all the other prisons in *Little Dorrit*, and the icy Essex marshes in *Great Expectations* are others. All these different places are used with a purpose, for which you should be alert in writing about any Victorian novel.

Interpretation and critical perspectives

Part 4: Critical approaches discussed some of the different ways in which critics in the past, and today, have approached the business of interpreting the Victorian novel. It is important to remember that there is no one 'right' way of responding to, or evaluating, any text. For instance, the references above to the author's 'message' will be regarded as provocative or old-fashioned by critics who place more emphasis on the reader's response than on the writer's 'intention'. It is important to be clear about your own perspectives – and about the possible perspectives of other readers – when writing about any Victorian novel.

Essentially (and this is an appropriate point with which to bring this discussion to a conclusion) it is a matter of context. A novel such as *Villette* by Charlotte Brontë can be studied in a variety of contexts – Gothic, feminist, psychological – and the conclusions you reach about the book may differ depending on the perspective from which you view it. The frequency with which Victorian novelists brought their stories to an unresolved or ambiguous ending (*Villette* itself, for instance, or *Great Expectations* or Hardy's *The Return of the Native*) is a reminder that in fiction, and in critical discussion, conclusions are rarely final. In writing about the Victorian novel, you too will find that the sheer scope, variety and vitality of the genre ensure that the last word is never said.

Assignments

1   Compare the stages through which the central characters pass in any two Victorian novels with which you are familiar.

2   Novelists are often critics of the society about which they write. Discuss how far the novelists whose work you have studied seem to be at odds with the prevailing values of their time.

3   By contrast with the previous assignment, consider whether any novelists whose work you know seem to express and endorse 'Victorian values'. Does your reading of 19th-century fiction help to give you a clear picture of what these values were, or not?

4   'The novelist's art is a highly serious criticism of life expressed in terms of comedy.' Discuss this view with reference to any two Victorian novels (whether essentially comic or otherwise) you know.

5   Discuss some of the ways in which Victorian novelists explore the issues of class and gender in their books. How different might a 21st-century perspective on these issues be?

6   Compare the various ways in which women are portrayed in at least two different novels you have read. Does the gender of the author (or the reader) have any bearing on the way you respond to the presentation of the women characters?

7   Try to write a review of a Victorian novel as it might have been written when the book first appeared.

8   Working in a group, or on your own, select a novel and see how easily it could be adapted – either into a film or a television serial. How would the plot have to be simplified or modified? Alternatively, examine closely a filmed or dramatised version of a Victorian novel to work out what were the gains and losses in transposing it from one medium to another.

9   It is the strength of narrative in a novel that makes us want to read on. Choose any two novels that seem to you to have particularly strong story lines, and identify the elements in the narratives that make them compelling.

10 Go to an art gallery and look closely at some Victorian paintings (by the Pre-Raphaelite artists, for instance). Often painting of this period itself contains a narrative. What links could be drawn between the narrative techniques of each medium? Do any of the paintings depict situations that you can compare with incidents or events in the novels you have been reading?

6 | Resources

Alphabetical list of authors

Matthew Arnold (1822–1888) Major Victorian poet, who recorded much of the unease of the period.

Jeremy Bentham (1748–1832) Philosopher, father of the Utilitarian school ('Benthamism').

Charlotte Brontë (1816–1855) Daughter of the Revd. Patrick Brontë, vicar of Haworth; sister of Emily and Anne; author of *Jane Eyre, Shirley, Villette, The Professor*. Married her father's curate, Arthur Nicholls (1854).

Emily Brontë (1818–1848) Sister of Charlotte and Anne; mystic and poet; author of *Wuthering Heights*.

Anne Brontë (1820–1849) Sister of Emily and Charlotte; author of *Agnes Grey* and *The Tenant of Wildfell Hall*.

Samuel Butler (1835–1902) Author of *The Way of All Flesh* (published posthumously).

Thomas Carlyle (1795–1881) Victorian sage, and historian; one of the most influential thinkers of the period. Satirised by Trollope (in *The Warden*) as Dr Pessimist Anticant.

Wilkie Collins (1824–1889) Author of *The Woman in White, The Moonstone*, etc.

Joseph Conrad (1857–1924) A Polish novelist who wrote in English. Author of *The Nigger of the 'Narcissus'*, 'Heart of Darkness', *Nostromo*, etc.

Dinah Craik (Mrs Craik) See Mulock.

Charles Dickens (1812–1870) Author of *Pickwick Papers, Oliver Twist, David Copperfield, Bleak House, Hard Times, Little Dorrit, Great Expectations, Our Mutual Friend*, etc.

Benjamin Disraeli (1804–1881) Conservative Prime Minister, later Lord Beaconsfield. Author of *Sybil, Lothair*, etc.

George Eliot (1819–1880) Born Mary Anne Evans. Common law marriage with George Henry Lewes (1854–1878); married J.W. Cross (1880). Author of *Adam Bede, The Mill on the Floss, Silas Marner, Felix Holt, Middlemarch, Daniel Deronda*, etc.

Elizabeth Gaskell (1810–1865) Contributor to Dickens' *Household Words* and *All the Year Round*. Author of *Mary Barton, Cranford, North and South,* etc. Biographer of Charlotte Brontë.

George Gissing (1857–1903) Author of *Born in Exile, The Odd Women,* etc.

Thomas Hardy (1840–1928) Author of *The Return of the Native, The Mayor of Casterbridge, The Woodlanders, Tess of the d'Urbervilles, Jude the Obscure,* etc.

Henry James (1843–1916) American novelist and critic who lived in Europe (naturalised British citizen 1915). Great influence on the English novel, both theory and form. Author of *The Portrait of a Lady, The Spoils of Poynton, The Wings of the Dove, The Golden Bowl,* etc.

Rudyard Kipling (1865–1936) Brought up in India. Author of *Stalky and Co., Kim,* etc.

Thomas Babington Macaulay (Lord Macaulay) (1800–1859) Historian who argued that national prosperity could be defined by the prosperity of the moneyed classes.

George Meredith (1828–1909) Author of *Beauchamp's Career, The Egoist,* etc.

John Stuart Mill (1806–1873) Philosopher and thinker.

Dinah Mulock (1826–1887) Published mostly under married name, Mrs Craik. Author of *John Halifax, Gentleman,* etc.

John Henry Newman (1801–1890) Cardinal; one of the founding figures of the Oxford Movement; converted to Roman Catholic church 1845. Author of *Loss and Gain,* etc.

'Mark Rutherford' (1831–1913) Pseudonym of William Hale White. Author of *The Autobiography of Mark Rutherford, Mark Rutherford's Deliverance,* etc.

William Makepeace Thackeray (1811–1863) Author of *Vanity Fair, Pendennis, The Newcomes,* etc.

Anthony Trollope (1815–1882) Author of *The Warden, Barchester Towers, Framley Parsonage, Phineas Finn, The Eustace Diamonds, The Way We Live Now, The Prime Minister,* etc.

Mary Augusta Ward (1851–1920) Better known as Mrs Humphry Ward. Granddaughter of Thomas Arnold of Rugby and niece of Matthew Arnold. Author of *Robert Elsmere, Helbeck of Bannisdale,* etc.

Charlotte Yonge (1823–1901) Novelist of the Oxford Movement. Author of *The Heir of Redclyffe, The Daisy Chain,* etc.

Chronology of texts and writers discussed

(The dates given are those of first appearance in book form.)

1830s	Charles Dickens	*Pickwick Papers* (1837)
		Oliver Twist (1838)
		Nicholas Nickleby (1839)
1840s	Charles Dickens	*The Old Curiosity Shop* (1841)
	Thomas Carlyle	*Past and Present* (1843)
	Charles Dickens	*Martin Chuzzlewit* (1844)
	Benjamin Disraeli	*Sybil* (1845)
	Charlotte Brontë	*Jane Eyre* (1847)
	Emily Brontë	*Wuthering Heights* (1847)
	Anne Brontë	*The Tenant of Wildfell Hall* (1848)
	William Thackeray	*Vanity Fair* (1848)
	Elizabeth Gaskell	*Mary Barton* (1848)
	John Henry Newman	*Loss and Gain* (1848)
1850s	Charles Dickens	*David Copperfield* (1850)
	William Thackeray	*Pendennis* (1850)
	Charles Dickens	*Bleak House* (1853)
	Elizabeth Gaskell	*Cranford* (1853)
	Charlotte Yonge	*The Heir of Redclyffe* (1853)
	Charlotte Brontë	*Villette* (1853)
	Charles Dickens	*Hard Times* (1854)
	Anthony Trollope	*The Warden* (1855)
	William Thackeray	*The Newcomes* (1855)
	Elizabeth Gaskell	*North and South* (1855)
	Charlotte Yonge	*The Daisy Chain* (1856)
	Dinah Mulock (Mrs Craik)	*John Halifax, Gentleman* (1857)
	Anthony Trollope	*Barchester Towers* (1857)
	Charles Dickens	*Little Dorrit* (1857)
	George Eliot	*Scenes of Clerical Life* (1858)
		Adam Bede (1859)
1860s	Charlotte Yonge	*Hopes and Fears* (1860)
	George Eliot	*The Mill on the Floss* (1860)
	Wilkie Collins	*The Woman in White* (1860)
	Charles Dickens	*Great Expectations* (1861)
	George Eliot	*Romola* (1863)
	Antony Trollope	*Can You Forgive Her?* (1864)
	Charles Dickens	*Our Mutual Friend* (1865)
	George Eliot	*Felix Holt* (1866)
	Wilkie Collins	*The Moonstone* (1868)
	Anthony Trollope	*Phineas Finn* (1869)

1870s	Benjamin Disraeli	*Lothair* (1870)
	George Eliot	*Middlemarch* (1872)
	Thomas Hardy	*Under the Greenwood Tree* (1872)
	Anthony Trollope	*The Eustace Diamonds* (1873)
	Thomas Hardy	*Far from the Madding Crowd* (1874)
		The Return of the Native (1874)
	Anthony Trollope	*The Way We Live Now* (1875)
		The Prime Minister (1876)
	George Eliot	*Daniel Deronda* (1876)
	Thomas Hardy	*The Return of the Native* (1878)
	George Meredith	*Beauchamp's Career* (1876)
		The Egoist (1879)
1880s	William Hale White	*The Autobiography of Mark Rutherford* (1881)
	('Mark Rutherford')	
	J.H. Shorthouse	*John Inglesant* (1881)
	William Hale White	*Mark Rutherford's Deliverance* (1885)
	Henry Rider Haggard	*King Solomon's Mines* (1885)
	Walter Pater	*Marius the Epicurean* (1885)
	Thomas Hardy	*The Mayor of Casterbridge* (1886)
	Henry Rider Haggard	*Allan Quartermain* (1887)
		She (1887)
	Thomas Hardy	*The Woodlanders* (1887)
	Mrs Humphry Ward	*Robert Elsmere* (1888)
1890s	Thomas Hardy	*Tess of the d'Urbervilles* (1891)
	George Gissing	*Born in Exile* (1892)
		The Odd Women (1893)
	Thomas Hardy	*Jude the Obscure* (1896)
	Rudyard Kipling	*Stalky and Co.* (1899)
1900s	Rudyard Kipling	*Kim* (1901)
	Joseph Conrad	'Heart of Darkness' (1902)
	Samuel Butler	*The Way of All Flesh* (1903, written 1873)

Further reading

In the *Icon Critical Guides* series (Icon Books, Cambridge): *Wuthering Heights* (ed. Patsy Stoneman, 1998); *Great Expectations* (ed. Nicholas Tredell, 1998); *Adam Bede*, *The Mill on the Floss* and *Middlemarch* (ed. Lucie Armitt, 2000)
The series is a guide to key critical material on major works. Covers the contemporary response and demonstrates the major critical developments of the 20th century.

In *The Critics Debate* series (Macmillan, London): *Hard Times* (ed. Allen Samuels, 1992) and *Wuthering Heights* (ed. Peter Miles, 1990)
This series introduces students to a variety of critical approaches to specific texts.

Arnold Kettle *An Introduction to the English Novel* (Hutchinson, 1951)
F.R. Leavis *The Great Tradition* (Chatto and Windus, 1948)
Dorothy Van Ghent *The English Novel* (Harper and Row, 1961)
Groundbreaking analyses of the Victorian novel, as discussed in Part 4.

Kenneth Graham *English Criticism of the Novel, 1865–1900* (Oxford, 1965)
Richard Stang *The Theory of the Novel in England, 1850–1870* (Oxford, 1959)
Standard accounts of the development of Victorian criticism of the novel.

J.B. Bullen (ed.) *Writing and Victorianism* (London, 1997)
Interdisciplinary in its approach – explores literary topics from a variety of perspectives.

Barbara Dennis & David Skilton (eds.) *Reform and Intellectual Debate in Victorian England* (Routledge, 1987)
A useful anthology, with notes and commentary, on the intellectual background of the novel.

Shirley Foster *Victorian Women's Fiction* (Croom Helm, 1985)
A close reading of the women novelists, major and minor.

Josephine Guy *The Victorian Social-Problem Novel* (Macmillan, 1996)
Focuses on the intellectual context, with close readings of *Hard Times*, *Mary Barton*, *Sybil*, etc.

W.E. Houghton *The Victorian Frame of Mind* (Yale, 1957)
Comprehensive and authoritative study of the literature that formed the Victorian mind.

Patricia Ingham *The Language of Gender and Class: Transformation in the Victorian Novel* (Routledge, 1996)
Looks closely at novels by the Brontës, Eliot, Gaskell, Dickens, Hardy, etc. to investigate stereotypes of gender and class.

Suzanne Keen *Victorian Renovations of the Novel* (Cambridge, 1998)
A study of narrative techniques in Victorian novels.

Kathleen Tillotson *Novels of the Eighteen Forties* (Oxford, 1954)
Selects novels by Charlotte Brontë, Thackeray, etc. and sets them in context of date of composition.

Herbert F. Tucker (ed.) *A Companion to Victorian Literature and Culture* (Blackwell's, 1999)
A very helpful introduction and reference book.

Michael Wheeler *English Fiction of the Victorian Period, 1830–1890* (Longman 1985, 1994)
Traces the development of the novel, with particular reference to Dickens, Thackeray, the Brontës, Hardy, etc.

Raymond Williams *Culture and Society* (Chatto and Windus, 1958)
Authoritative survey of Victorian and 20th-century culture, with useful chapters on the industrial novel.

Websites
The following site is an indispensable source of current information on every important publication from 1945 to 1999 on every field of 19th-century British studies:

www.victoriandatabase.com

Glossary

Technical terms

Bildungsroman German term signifying 'novel of education or development' (Bildung = formation). *Great Expectations* and *Pendennis* are good examples.

Canon a list of books or writings regarded as representing the texts which authentically define an area of literature, either on grounds of historical importance, literary merit or influence, etc.

Didactic aiming to teach (or preach).

Discourse traditionally, any sustained writing or speaking (discussion) on a given theme or topic, or on a range of such themes and topics; however, a text can also be analysed in terms of its 'discourse' – the perspectives it adopts and the values (implicit and explicit) that it projects.

Genre although genre is often used loosely to refer to prose, poetry and drama as the three main forms of literary writing, it has a more specific meaning. Types of writing such as the gothic novel or industrial novel can be described as genres, identifying a group of texts that share key features of form, theme or approach.

Ideology generally, the characteristic manner of thinking associated with a class or individual (e.g. bourgeois ideology); as a term in Marxist literary criticism it refers to the system of ideas at the core of political or economic theory.

Narrative device a technique by which the narrative of a novel is conveyed to the reader. It includes the use of the omniscient narrator who 'knows' the plot and directs the novel from the wings, whose personality may be deliberately suppressed or may be assumed as a deliberate intention by the author (as in the novels of, for instance, George Eliot, Trollope, Thackeray). Another example of the narrative device is the first-person narrator.

Omniscient narrator see Narrative device.

Persona a voice or character adopted by a writer.

Realism a term which first came to England from France in the 1850s. Realism meant the replication in art (of whatever kind) of all the commonplace details of human experience, which would be familiar to the reader or viewer, who could verify it by reference to his/her own experience. Later in the century the term shifted in meaning: realism no longer merely recorded minutiae, but became the intensifying of experience.

Symbolism a mode of discourse which, instead of referring to something directly, refers to it indirectly through the medium of something else.

Historical terms and events

Anglo-Catholic/High Church see Oxford Movement.

Boer Wars British wars in South Africa in 1881 and 1899–1902 against the Boers (Dutch-descended South Africans).

Chartist Movement working-class movement officially launched in 1838. The Chartists drafted their demands into a bill of six points, the 'People's Charter'. Petitions were rejected by Parliament in 1839 and again in 1842. A third petition in 1848 ended in ridicule and the transportation of Chartist leaders.

Crimean War war fought against Russia from 1854–1856 by Britain, France and Austria. One heroine was Florence Nightingale who established hospital and nursing facilities for wounded soldiers.

Dissenters members of Nonconformist churches outside the Church of England, for example Methodists, Baptists and Unitarians.

Education Acts before the Education Act of 1833 made £20,000 available for state education, no state aid had been given to schools. Primary education for the poor began to be compulsory with the Forster Education Act of 1870.

Evangelicals/Low Church another party in the Church of England, which emphasised the authority of the Bible rather than the sacraments.

Jingoistic something aggressively patriotic. The word came from a music hall song in 1877 when Disraeli ordered the fleet to Constantinople to aid the Turks against the Russians ('We don't want to fight, but by Jingo if we do ...').

Laissez-faire a policy whereby government does not interfere in economic affairs, but allows trade to look after itself.

Manchester School a name given to business men who advocated a policy of Free Trade, in other words trade unrestricted by custom duties.

Nonconformist a Protestant person or sect who/which does not conform to the doctrines of the Church of England, for example Methodist, Baptist, Congregationalist.

Oxford Movement movement led by Newman, Keble and Pusey to re-catholicise the Church of England. First stage, wholly concerned with dogma, lasted about twelve years (1833–1845), and ended with the conversion of Newman to the Roman Catholic Church; the second stage (about 1850–1880) was increasingly concerned with ritual.

Poor Law Amendment Act parish relief was replaced in 1834 by the Union workhouse system, whereby the Union poorhouse was made more unattractive than the situation of the poorest labourer, and inhuman rules enforced (see *Oliver Twist*).

Reform Bills the Great Reform Bill of 1832 altered both franchise and representation. It increased electorate only to the richer middle classes, but was significant in the precedent created. The Second Reform Bill (1867) gave the vote to most of the middle class, enfranchising all householders, and extra parliamentary seats were given to new industrial towns. The Third Reform Bill (1884) slightly increased the electorate and re-distributed seats further.

Test Acts Acts of Parliament intended to disqualify Nonconformists and Roman Catholics from public office.

Tractarians another name for followers of the Oxford Movement.

Utilitarianism equated material prosperity and moral health, and worked on the principle of its most notable spokesman, Jeremy Bentham, that the ultimate end of human conduct was 'the greatest happiness of the greatest number'. Famous attack on Utilitarianism by Dickens in *Hard Times*; nonetheless it was responsible for most of the Victorian reform programmes.

Whig and Tory Parties loose groupings of British politicians which developed in the 18th and early 19th centuries as parliamentary politics assumed ever greater importance. The two names originated as terms of abuse that subsequently 'stuck', and were the precursors of the Liberal and Conservative Parties respectively. Whigs tended towards more radical policies than their Tory, largely land-owning, counterparts.

Index